Pope John Paul II's Gospel of Work

WITH
INTRODUCTION AND COMMENTARY

D1600098

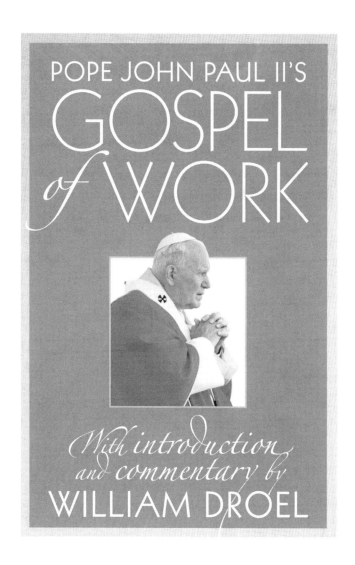

POPE JOHN PAUL II'S

GOSPEL
of WORK

With introduction and commentary by

WILLIAM DROEL

TWENTY THIRD *23rd*
PUBLICATIONS

John Paul II's talks and writings are here slightly edited for consistent pronouns. The pope sometimes spoke in the third person ("The pope...he..."); sometimes in the first person ("I...").

Likewise, the pope (at least in translation) interchangeably—even in the same paragraph—uses the term "man" (meaning, "mankind" or "humankind") and the term "people." The phrase "people are" (and the like) is used here, except when the term "man" or "mankind" better carries a familiar biblical phrase.

Cover photo provided by *Pope John Paul II Cultural Center* in Washington, D.C.

Twenty-Third Publications
A Division of Bayard
One Montauk Avenue, Suite 200
New London, CT 06320
(860) 437-3012 or (800) 321-0411
www.23rdpublications.com

Text from John Paul II © Libreria Editrice Vaticana.

ISBN 978-1-58595-585-5
Library of Congress Catalog Card Number: 2006920449
Printed in the U.S.A.

CONTENTS

Introduction

Catholic philosophy and theology, although greatly influenced by Aristotle and other ancient Greek philosophers, has never been comfortable with the Hellenistic contempt for work. The New Testament and early Christian writers, like St. Jerome, St. Augustine, and St. John Chrysostom, frequently allude to the religious value of work. It is true that during the Middle Ages the monks sometimes regarded work as only a backdrop to prayer, not exactly spiritual in and of itself. Yet those same monks witnessed to the dignity of work, never considering it servile. While many people refused the so-called indignities of dirty jobs, the Catholic monks in Europe joyfully drained swamps, constructed buildings, made beds, and swept hallways.

If strong strains in Catholicism sometimes regard work as strictly a penance for original sin or a necessary evil, other strains affirm that work has some Christian purpose by disposing people to prayer, by lifting the material world toward heaven, and by connecting workers to one another.

In recent years there has been a very positive turn in the Catholic doctrine on work.

Pope John XXIII, for example, grounds his 1963 encyclical *Pacem in Terris* in the image of God as Creator and the image of humankind as God's collaborators. The achievements of human work, John XXIII proclaims, are sacraments of the infinite great God who created the universe. In 1965 the world's Catholic bishops who assembled at Vatican II stated in *Gaudium et Spes* that the matter is settled: Human work "accords with God's will" and workers can "justly consider that by their labor they are unfolding the Creator's work…, and contributing by their personal industry to the realization in history of the divine plan."

It could be argued that some of the most significant developments in the modern Catholic theology of work took place in Poland, and that the new "gospel of work," as developed by the Polish pope, should be considered near the top of the achievements of John Paul II's life.

It should be no surprise that John Paul II continually preached a "gospel of work" and repeatedly called for "a spirituality of work" and "a civilization based on work"—evocative phrases, the full implications of which will continue to unfold in coming years. John Paul II was, after all, a worker! He and St. Peter, two of the four popes who served at least twenty-five years, are also among those popes who held a workaday job.

St. Peter, of course, was a fisherman. At age twenty, Karol Wojtyla was a delivery boy for a restaurant in downtown Krakow. During the Nazi occupation he labored on public works projects, including a school building. He worked as a stonecutter in a limestone quarry and from 1942-44 in the Solvay Chemical Plant where he repaired railroad tracks, served as a train brakeman, handled explosives, and more. He was, as early as age fifteen, a theater promoter, translator of classic dramas, a playwright, director, and actor. He was a philosophy teacher fluent in the Marxist perspective on work.

John Paul II also learned about work through workers' movements in Poland (most famously, *Solidarnosc*, but before that the Committee for the Defense of Workers). Earlier in Marseilles, Paris, and Brussels, he met worker-priests and Catholic Action leaders. Additionally, several Poles influenced John Paul II's thinking on work, including Father Jozef Tischner, a Krakow philosopher; Bodhan Cywinski, a Warsaw activist in the Committee for the Defense of Workers; the nineteenth-century poet Cyprian Kamil Norwid, who wrote about work and redemption; Father Jan Piwowarczyk, the rector of Wojtyla's underground seminary who taught distributive justice and progressive social policies; Father Jan Badeni, SJ, a chaplain to groups of Catholic workers; Father Andrzej Szymanski who studied Marxism; and Jerzy Turowicz, editor of *Universal Weekly* and the monthly *Znak*, to which Wojtyla contributed.

In particular, John Paul II drew upon his mentor Cardinal Stefan Wyszynski's 1946 *Duch Pracy Ludzkiej* (literally, *The Spirit of People's*

Work, now available in English as *Working Your Way to Heaven*, Sophia Institute Press). In that book, Wyszynski heaves aside the common mistake that work is the result of original sin: "Even before the fall people had to work, for they had to dress paradise," he writes. "Work is therefore the duty of people from the first day of life. It is not the result of original sin; it is not a punishment for disobedience."

John Paul II uses this fresh interpretation of the Adam and Eve story in his book *Sign of Contradiction* to celebrate God as Creator, God as worker. John Paul II, almost obsessed with Genesis, draws attention to the opportunity for people through their work to be God's artisans for an improved world, a new humanity.

In hundreds of talks and sermons, in his poems and in his writings, especially in the 1981 encyclical *Laborem Exercens*, John Paul II develops several themes in the *gospel of work*.

For example, he presumes that in a true civilization of work everyone will wear with pride the title "worker." In most societies today this is not the case. For example, magazines geared toward "working women" routinely slight homemakers by featuring only paid workers—as if homemaking is not work. Corporation executives, lawyers, and others in skyscraper offices snobbishly eschew the label "worker," using other descriptions like "professional." Likewise, a reviewer once called the title of a Catholic booklet, *Unemployed Workers*, an oxymoron. The reviewer presumably had never performed the hard work of finding a job.

What gives work its dignity, John Paul II says, is not the type of work being done but the fact that the worker is a human being who is participating in God's ongoing creative activity and God's saving activity. A spirituality of work, he says, "does away with the very basis of the ancient differentiation of people into classes according to the kind of work done."

The dignity of the title "worker" was made graphic at the 1984 funeral of John Paul II's countryman, Father Jerzy Popieluszko, a martyr for the Solidarity movement. The thousands who attended that funeral came dressed in the garb of their occupations—as coal miners, construction workers, doctors, and others. They had come as workers to honor an outspoken supporter of a workers' union.

The solidarity among the mourners at the Popieluszko funeral also brought home another theme of John Paul II: The world of work is more than an individual affair. In refreshing contrast to the highly individualistic rhetoric and ritual of work, John Paul II insists that work creates bonds of solidarity among coworkers and between workers and others in the community. "Do not forget," he once told business leaders in Barcelona, "that the primary characteristic of labor is that of uniting humanity." Therefore, in the divine economy there is no such thing as strictly private ownership. "Each person is fully entitled," says John Paul II, to be considered "a part-owner of the great workbench."

According to John Paul II, work can never be regarded as simply a necessary means to achieving private ends. People work not just to get money with which to buy more things. The real virtue of work is to allow people to become fully human. John Paul II tries to express this notion with his easily misunderstood "principle of the priority of labor over capital." He isn't taking sides in a union-management dispute (though he wholeheartedly supports the right to organize and the necessity of a labor movement in a free society). He is, rather, asserting that each worker should participate in the economy and share in the responsibility and creativity found at the *great workbench*. Furthermore, the work of each person and of each company must contribute not just to the owners but also to the whole society. That's an awesome challenge for our culture, which scoffs at the notion of *stakeholders* in business.

Through work, John Paul II explains, people share in God's ongoing creativity and collaborate with Christ "for the redemption of humanity." This is the implied meaning of the prayer over the eucharistic gifts at Mass: "We have this bread to offer; *which human hands have made*....We have this wine to offer, fruit of the vine and *work of human hands*." The bread offered at the altar, says John Paul II, refers not only to baked dough, or even to all the food that sustains our bodies. The altar bread made by human hands is also "the bread of science and progress, civilization and culture." The wine that is poured and shared at Mass represents all the fruits and vegetables harvested by migrant farm workers, transported by teamsters, stocked and sold by grocers. It also represents the fruit of justice, as negotiated daily by lawyers, police officers, community organizers, and legislators. The offertory gift that becomes the body and blood of Christ is our daily work—both at Mass and in the places where Eucharist "lives"—in offices, hospitals, schools, neighborhoods, and homes during the week.

It is said that the Polish church is conservative. In its encounter with Communism and other forces, however, the Polish church—with leaders like Lech Walesa, John Paul II, and others—anticipated and advanced a liberation theology and practice, based on a Christian appreciation for work, which has greatly influenced the whole church and our world.

Years ago, in societies where people were unquestionably Catholic and where the hierarchy had direct influence on government and business, evangelization of the laity might have been a low priority. That's not the situation in many places today. Christians in a pluralistic society need a perspective on their day-to-day surroundings; that is, modern Christians need a philosophy and theology of work. Without some theology that speaks to the workweek, as John Paul II prophetically senses, most lay people will relegate their faith to Sunday morning and to private piety. Meanwhile, the wider culture can easily drift away from the best aspirations of humankind. John Paul II, drawing constructive lessons from his experiences with Communism and other ideologies, was on the cutting edge of a dynamic relationship between faith and weekday life. He was a greatly admired pope, a person of very substantial accomplishments, and is a saint for our time.

John Paul II's social vision continues to be the primary agenda for our Church: finding a mutually beneficial way to engage the modern world. It's a big, complex agenda. John Paul II's "gospel of work" is, as he said, "the fundamental key" to that agenda. Unfortunately, a dynamic theology of work is not yet a salient feature in the spirituality of most Catholics—at least that's my observation from my cluttered attic office near Chicago's Midway Airport, and I suspect my observation applies also to Chicago's north side, to Boston and to Seattle, to Poland, to Western Europe, and to other continents. To carry out a legacy for John Paul II, Catholics and others will among other things have to get more serious about the present vocation crisis in many occupations and professions. It is a crisis of meaning in which *careerism* is substituted for *calling*. It is a crisis in which many jobs are not structured for health and meaningfulness but for profit. It is a crisis about the quality of work, about ethical practices in the marketplace, about poverty amid plenty.

Catholicism, says John Paul II, "has given a religious meaning to work and recognizes the spiritual value of technological progress. There is no vocation more religious than work."

"I want to remind workers," John Paul II told a 1982 gathering in Gabon, "that there exists *a gospel of work*, that is to say, that the vocation of human beings is to subdue the earth and to realize themselves as persons in this way." Through work, "small and great, people who are inventive, courageous, passionately fond of their work, and desirous of sharing the fruits of their labor" participate in God's ongoing creation. Work also has "mysterious value as a sharing in the redeeming work of Christ, through the silent offering of fatigues that are part of work." Without a gospel of work, John Paul II concludes, it is "impossible for people to become more human."

How to Use This Book

This book is a contribution to an ongoing conversation about business ethics, spirituality in business, faith in daily life, the meaning of work, and the like. This general topic is often reduced to an examination of individual behavior—important as personal integrity and good example are. A major theme of this book, however, is the insistence that excellence at work must address the moral worth of systems, institutions, policies, and, as appropriate, capitalism itself.

With that in mind, this book can be read by anyone who admires Pope John Paul II or anyone who is interested in workplace issues or management theories. This book achieves its wider goal when it is discussed in groups. It could be assigned in management, philosophy, or religious studies courses. This book would be best used for group discussion—maybe by an executive team at a company (not necessarily a Catholic company), maybe by colleagues that regularly gather for reflection, maybe by a Cursillo group, or maybe by a parish staff or a parish renewal group.

As in other sharing groups, one based on this book would prefer real-life examples over abstractions and hypothetical situations. Examples from one's own company or work life are more useful than secondhand accounts of someone else's experience. The purpose of the discussion is not to solve another person's dilemma—we are all adept at offering cheap advice. Rather, the purpose is to create a forum in which people feel comfortable simply sharing their difficulties and their achievements.

A discussion around this book has to be different from a gripe session. A participant in a full discussion of this book's themes will not simply return to his or her workweek with a "grin and bear" attitude about unacceptable situations. Nor will he or she ineffectively lash out at supervisors or coworkers. Slowly and incrementally a confident worker will, in concert with like-minded others, make positive changes in workplace habits or policies or even, on occasion, within a sector of an industry.

I am interested in joining any conversation that emerges from this book. I publish a monthly newsletter on faith and work. Please contact me with your reactions and your stories: Bill Droel, c/o National Center for the Laity (PO Box 291102, Chicago, IL 60629).

Hints for Starting a Support/Discussion Group

- A support group can be male, female, or mixed gender; it can include members from a single occupation or profession or it can be mixed. There is no magic composition.

- A support group should begin with a three-to-six session expectation. Most groups reach their depth of sharing within six sessions. If things feel right, renew the expectation for another six weeks or indefinitely. If not, disband the group without recrimination. If everyone else enjoys the group but you, drop out.

- A group must meet regularly, maybe weekly or monthly. At less than ten times per year it might be an enjoyable social gathering, but it is likely not a support group.

- The group needs some structure (maybe an opening prayer, a set question or two). It will collapse with no structure or under too much structure.

- Giving support is something different from giving advice or solving other people's problems.

- A successful group will include appropriate doses of prayer, intellectual exchange, personal sharing, and socializing. If it is all socializing, it might be worth continuing—just don't call it a support group.

- The group itself is not a change agent. The group might occasionally or seasonally get involved in a charitable project or issue a statement or letter to the editor. But the primary purpose of the group is to fortify and challenge its members as they go back into their normal institutions.

Thoughts from a Working Person's Saint

Excerpts from talks, statements, and poems of Pope John Paul II

I Am a Worker

Christianity and the church have no fear of the world of work. We have no fear of the system based on work. I have no fear of working people. You have always been particularly close to me. I come from your midst. I come from the quarries of Zakrzowek, from the Solvay furnaces in Borek Falecki, and then from Nowa Huta. Through all these surroundings, through my own experience of work, I boldly say that I learned the gospel anew. I noticed and became convinced that the problems being raised today about human labor are deeply engraved in the gospel, that those problems cannot be fully solved without the gospel.

— Homily in Nowa Huta, Poland, July 1979

I do not forget the difficult years of the World War during which I myself had direct experience of physical work such as yours, of daily toil and its dependence, its heaviness and monotony. I shared the necessities of workers, their rightful demands, and their legitimate aspirations. I know very well that work should not alienate and frustrate, but should correspond to people's higher dignity. I can testify to one thing: in the most difficult moments we Polish workers found in our faith in God, in our confidence in the Blessed Virgin Mother of God, in the ecclesial community united around its pastors, a light greater than the darkness, and an unshakable hope.

— Talk in Monterrey, Mexico, January 1979

My experience had not been that of a worker-priest [as such], but of a worker-seminarian. Having worked with my hands, I knew quite well the meaning of physical labor. Every day I [was] with people who did heavy work. I came to know their living situations, their families, their interests, their human worth, and their dignity. I personally experienced many kindnesses from them.

— AUTOBIOGRAPHY *GIFT AND MYSTERY*, 1996

Poem for a Deceased "Companion of Labor" in the Quarry

He wasn't alone.
His muscles grew into the flesh of the crowd, energy their pulse,
As long as they held a hammer, as long as his feet felt the ground.
And a stone smashed his temples and cut through
  his heart's chamber.
They took his body and walked in a silent line
Toil still lingered about him, a sense of wrong.
They wore gray shirts, boots ankle-deep in mud.
In this, they showed the end.
How violently his time halted: the pointers on the
  low voltage dials jerked, then dropped to zero again.
White stone now within him, eating into his being,
  taking over enough of him to turn him into stone.
Who will lift up that stone, unfurl his thoughts again
  under the cracked temples?
So plaster cracks on the wall.
They laid him down, his back on a sheet of gravel.
His wife came, worn out with worry; his son returned from school.
Should his anger now flow into the anger of others?
It was maturing in him through his own truth and love.

Should he be used by those who came after, deprived of substance,
unique and deeply his own?
The stones on the move again; a wagon bruising the flowers.
Again the electric current cuts deep into the walls.
But the man has taken with him the world's inner structure,
where the greater the anger, the higher the explosion of love.

— "The Quarry," 1956

FOR REFLECTION

"I learned the gospel anew through my work."

There is no such thing as free-floating, stand-alone religious faith. Faith is always embedded in culture and experience. Even hermits process their faith out of or in reaction to a particular culture.

- Have you seen your parents at work? What was their attitude about work?

- How does your upbringing, your ethnicity, and your parents' lives affect your reception of Christianity?

- Some products bear a tag or label "Made in the USA." Is there a work culture "made in the USA" that colors our business conduct irrespective of the intentions of individual workers?

- Once in a while we hear the phrase "taking my faith to work." But think about this: How does the North American culture of work influence your take on faith?

- Is there a sense in which you can, in John Paul II's phrase, "learn the gospel anew" through your job, your extended family, and your civic involvements?

THE MEANING OF WORK

Work is the fundamental dimension of our life on earth. Work has a significance that is not merely technical but ethical....Work must help people become better, more mature spiritually, more responsible, in order that each worker might realize a vocation on earth both as an unrepeatable person and in community with others, especially in the fundamental community constituted by the family.

— HOMILY AT JANSA GORA, POLAND, JUNE 1979

Work is good for us. Through work we not only transform nature, adapting it to our needs, but we also achieve fulfillment as human beings and indeed in a sense become more human.

— HOMILY IN MONTEREY, CALIFORNIA, SEPTEMBER 1987

Work must not be a mere necessity, but it must be considered a real vocation, a call from God to build a new world in which justice and brotherhood dwell, a foretaste of the kingdom of God, in which there will certainly not be shortages or limitations. Work must be the means by which the whole of creation will be subjected to the dignity of the human being and Son of God. Work offers the opportunity to commit oneself with the whole community without resentment, without bitterness, without hatred, but with the universal love of Christ that excludes no one and embraces everyone.

— TALK IN GUADALAJARA, MEXICO, JANUARY 1979

I come to announce the gospel of work to you, dearest men and women workers, present and absent, those born on this land and those coming from other areas....The church believes it has an unavoidable duty in the social field to help fortify the human community according to the divine law by recalling the dignity and rights of workers, by stigmatizing situations where such rights are violated, and by favoring [economic] exchanges leading to authentic progress for workers and for society.

During the first four years of my pontificate, I have unceasingly proclaimed the centrality of humankind...insisting on people's primacy over things and the importance of the subjective dimension of work, based on the dignity of the human person.

— Talk in Barcelona, Spain, November 1982

Through work people not only transform nature, adapting it to their needs, but also *achieve fulfillment* as human beings and indeed, in a sense, become more human. Without this consideration it is impossible to understand industriousness [and other work virtues].

— Encyclical *Laborem Exercens*, September 1981

It must be said over and over again that work is for people, not people for work. People are indeed the true purpose of the whole process of production. Every consideration of the value of work must begin with the worker, and every solution proposed to the problems of the social order must recognize the primacy of the human person over things....The worker is always more important than profits and machines.

— Talk in Sydney, Australia, November 1986

FOR REFLECTION

"Work is for people; not people for work."

Work is a vocation. It is something that you do to glorify God. A vocation is not just personal ambition. It is matching your unique gifts to objective needs in the family and in society. The process of discerning society's needs and your gifts and then matching the two is facilitated by your family, your school, your associations; that is, when our institutions are functioning properly.

- When you go to the store when and how are you aware that your exchange of money for goods or services is an exchange of gifts and talents? What might you do to increase this awareness? Do you appreciate that the normal division of labor is the most basic form of ministry? Discuss what this means to you.

- How is the design of God planted or embedded within your work—its raw materials, its design, its normal procedures?

- How is the design of God planted within the subjects of your work? How are people respected at your office, your school, your union hall, your clinic, your community organization, or your family gathering? Do you sometimes encounter situations where "people are made for work" rather than "work is structured for people"?

- How are you teaching your children that their worldly pursuits matter to God? Are you confident that their mentors at school and elsewhere are teaching them that work is a form of Christian service?

WORK, CREATION, AND REDEMPTION

From Genesis to Joseph's Carpenter Shop to the Cross

Work corresponds to God's design and will. The first pages of Genesis present creation to us as the work of God, God's labor. So to be like God, God calls on many to work. Hence, work is not something off on the side. Even less is it a curse from heaven. On the contrary, work is a primordial blessing from the Creator, an activity permitting people to realize themselves and to offer service to society. In addition, a worker will have a higher reward, for your toil is not in vain when it is done in the Lord….

When understood in this way, work is not a biological necessity for the sake of subsistence, but a moral duty. It is an act of love and it turns into joy, the deep joy of giving oneself through work to one's own family and to others, the intimate joyousness of offering oneself to God and of serving humankind, even though such giving entails sacrifices. Thus Christian work has a paschal meaning.

— Talk in Barcelona, Spain, November 1982

The Son of God became man and worked with human hands. Work then has a dignity of its own in God's plan for creation. We hear in the very first pages of Genesis that we were created "in the image of God…male and female." Entrusting the whole universe to us, God told us to "be fruitful and multiply, and fill the earth and subdue it." So we know, not only by reason alone but through revelation, that through their work people share in the Creator's work. We continue it and, in a sense, perfect it by our own work, our toil, by daily effort to wrest a livelihood from the earth, or from the sea, or by applying energy to the many different processes of production. How noble is this mission that only we—by our work—can realize!

Indeed, we Christians are convinced that the achievements of the human race—in art, science, culture, and technology—are a sign of God's greatness and the flowering of God's mysterious design.

Jesus himself gave particular emphasis to this truth: that through work, people share in the activity of the Creator. For Jesus was himself a workingman, a craftsman like Joseph of Nazareth. Jesus clearly belonged to the working world. So did most of his disciples and listeners: ordinary fishermen, farmers, and workers. So when he speaks about the kingdom of God, Jesus constantly uses terms connected with human work: the work of the shepherd, the farmer, the doctor, the sower, the householder, the servant, the steward, the fisherman, the merchant, the laborer. And he compares the building up of God's kingdom to the manual work of harvesters and fishermen.

— TALK IN PUSAN, SOUTH KOREA, MAY 1984

The law of the cross is engraved on our work. It is with the sweat of his brow that the farmer works. It is with the sweat of his brow that the ironworker works. It is with the sweat of his brow—the terrible sweat of death—that Christ agonizes on the cross....Christ had himself put on the cross, as if on the great threshold of spiritual history, to oppose any form of degradation, including degradation by work....This must be remembered by the worker and the employer.

— HOMILY IN NOWA HUTA, POLAND, JUNE 1979

Enter the house of Nazareth, approach this workbench where, beside Joseph and under the maternal glance of his mother, the Son of God worked. God-made-man knew the experience of human work. We want to enter there, into this house of Nazareth. We want to bring all the modern problems of work: all the social, economic, political, cultural, and moral problems, all the anxieties connected with the world of work, especially the worry caused by unemployment....In this house in Nazareth we return close to Jesus the worker.... There cannot be human work that is alienated [here]. I say this in the name of Jesus....Human work is redeemed, is restored in Jesus Christ.

— Angelus Prayer in the Vatican, March 1984

People eat the bread produced by the work of human hands— and this means not only the daily bread that keeps the body alive but also the bread of science and progress, civilization and culture. It is also a perennial truth that people eat this bread by the sweat of their brow, that is to say, not only by personal effort and toil but also in the midst of many tensions, conflicts, and crises, which, in relationship to the reality of work, disturb the life of society and also all humanity.... People, created in the image of God, share by their work in the activity of the Creator....By enduring the toil of work in union with Christ crucified for us, people in a way collaborate with the Son of God for the redemption of humanity.

— Encyclical *Laborem Exercens*, September 1981

FOR REFLECTION

"Work is not a curse nor something off on the side."

At times our tradition has implied that work is a punishment for Adam and Eve's original sin. But listen to John Paul II: The very first pages of Genesis tell us that work is a fundamental dimension of our existence. Far from being a punishment, work is the way we participate in God's ongoing creation. Although it involves sweat and toil, work is a blessing.

- Is John Paul II naïve? That is, doesn't your work (the daily grind on the job, around the house, and in the neighborhood) feel like a punishment for sin?

Some people criticize John Paul II for his emphasis on Genesis 1:28: "Fill the earth and have dominion over it." Or, as translated in the *Jerusalem Bible*: "Fill the earth and conquer it."
People are ruining the planet, these critics say. We don't need a "dominion theology." We need to hear about stewardship, another Old Testament theme.

- How do you exercise your dominion in your place of work, your home, your community? Does your use of power and your leadership conflict with your responsibility as a steward for your employees, your students, your clients, your children, or our planet? Why or why not?

John Paul II sees in Jesus' crucifixion a protest against all degradation in the workplace and in the economy.

- What does God nailed to a cross have to do with slavery, sweatshops, union busting, crooked scales and measures, dishonest business practices, and even rudeness in the shop or office? Is Jesus on the cross protesting anything at your place of work?

WORKERS AS CONSUMERS

It is not wrong to want to live better. What is wrong is a lifestyle that is presumed to *be* better when it is directed toward *having* rather than *being*, and which wants to have more, not in order to be more but in order to spend life in enjoyment as an end in itself. It is therefore necessary to create lifestyles in which the quest for truth, beauty, goodness, and communion with others for the sake of common growth are the factors that determine consumer choices, savings, and investments....

A given culture reveals its overall understanding of life through the choices it makes in production and consumption. It is here that the phenomenon of consumerism arises. In singling out new needs and new means to meet them, one must be guided by a comprehensive picture that represents all the dimensions of life and that subordinates material and instinctive dimensions to interior and spiritual ones....Of itself an economic system does not possess criteria for correctly distinguishing new and higher forms of satisfying human needs from artificial new needs, [those] which hinder the formation of a mature personality. Thus a great deal of educational and cultural work is urgently needed, including the education of consumers in the responsible use of their power of choice.

— ENCYCLICAL *CENTESIMUS ANNUS*, MAY 1991

[Work must be rescued] from the logic of profit, from the lack of solidarity, from the fever of earning ever more, from the desire to accumulate and consume [because when work] is subjected to inhumane wealth, it becomes a seductive and merciless idol....

[Liberation from consumerism] comes when there is a return to the austere words of the Divine Master: "For what does it profit a man if he gains the whole world and loses or forfeits himself?"

The Divine Worker of Nazareth reminds us that life is more than food and that work is for people, not people for work. What makes a life great is not the entity of gain, nor the type of profession, or the level of the career. People are worth more than the goods they produce or possess.

— Talk in Vatican City, May 2004

The church [has a] constant preoccupation with the delicate question of property ownership....

[The] voice of the church, echoing the voice of the human conscience, did not cease to make itself heard down through the centuries, amid the most varied sociocultural systems and circumstances. It deserves and needs to be heard in our age as well, when the growing affluence of a few people parallels the growing poverty of the masses. It is then that the church's teaching, which says there is a *social mortgage* on all private property, takes on an urgent character.

— Address in Puebla, Mexico, January 1979

FOR REFLECTION

"There is a social mortgage on all private property."

Christians are not expected to be ascetics, though several notable Christians have chosen that path. We must, however, balance our freedom to acquire something with the opportunity each new thing gives us to improve society, even if "society" for that moment is our children or elderly relatives. People are motivated through the right to hold property privately, says Catholic social teaching. But that property, which was once held exclusively by God, is ultimately destined for a common purpose. John Paul II calls this process "the common purpose of goods" or "the universal destination of material goods." He reminds us too about "distributive justice," the duty of government and other authorities to regulate work and commerce in the interest of the common good.

- When you buy something, do you ever consider how your control of this item will benefit your family, your neighbors, your employees, or others? Discuss what this means for your purchases.

- Do you shop in order to "have more" or do you normally shop in order "to be more"? Give an example of each from your own life.

- Do you ever get irritated with government rules or inspections regarding wages, workplace safety, unemployment, and the like?

THE CHURCH'S MISSION
IS TO THE WORLD OF WORK

It is your duty, dear priests, to see to it that [the church's] wish comes true, so that the gap between church and factory begins to fill, and that the fumes of incense mix with those of industries in rising up to heaven....The workers' situation should be reconsidered, to allow workers to be more human and to recover their true greatness as collaborators with God's creative work, by impressing the sign of God's industriousness upon the matter [at hand in the workplace].

— TALK TO PRIESTS IN THE VATICAN, APRIL 1979

I wish to converse with you [workers] in order to know your state of mind towards the church....The church, it is said, [only] concerns itself with moral and religious values and does not take an interest in economic and temporal values, as if it did not understand the reality of workers' situations. And so the words and well-meaning gestures of the church are doubted or distrusted. Some even ask themselves: What has religion got to do with industry, are these not two heterogeneous realities?

...I will answer you in all sincerity that these objections have no reason to exist, when we consider your activity [as Christian workers] and when one bears in mind the objectives to which your work is directed, that is, to human life in its entirety, in its dignity, and in its superior and immortal destiny....

The Christian element [of work], instead of arousing anxieties, makes it possible to overcome them because it brings peace, justice, and unity into the factory.

— Talk in Pomezia, Italy, September 1979

The church is convinced that work is a fundamental dimension of human existence on earth....The church considers it her duty to speak out on work....It is her particular duty to form a spirituality of work that will help *all* people to come closer, through work, to God....This Christian spirituality of work should be a heritage shared by *all*.

— Encyclical *Laborem Exercens*, September 1981

FOR REFLECTION

"A spirituality of work will help all people come closer, through work, to God."

We sometimes belittle the humdrum routines of family life, of the office, of neighborhood settings, or, in general, of the daily grind. Yet John Paul II tells us that the locus of our spirituality is our classroom, the corner store, the precinct, the clinic, our professional association, and more. Instead of understanding spirituality as something that an individual procures, like a consumer would, John Paul II proposes a spirituality that is present in our milieu, Monday through Saturday.

- How do you—both personally and through your institutions—affirm the world around you?

- Have you ever been aware of grace embedded in your place of work, your neighborhood, or your family life? Describe an occasion when that happened.

- People sometimes denounce defects in our culture. They can point the finger at sin. Have you ever tried to announce the presence of God in our culture, in your surroundings? How might you do that this week?

- How might your parish affirm homemakers, clerks, lawyers, or other specific occupations and worldly endeavors?

THE CHRISTIAN CONCEPT
OF ENTERPRISE

People and human values must be the beginning and end of the economy. [The standard for management decisions], even in the moments of major crisis cannot be an overvaluation of profit.

— TALK IN MILAN, ITALY, MAY 1983

I invite you to reflect on the Christian concept of enterprise. I would remind you that above all there is a deeper problem, above and beyond technical and economic aspects in which you [business leaders] are masters. I mean the moral dimension. Economics and technology really have no meaning unless they have reference to people, whom they must serve. Work is actually for people, not people for work. Likewise, enterprise is for people and not people for enterprise....

An enterprise is not just...a production structure. It should also transform itself into a life-giving community, a place where people live with and relate to their peers, where personal development is not only allowed but also encouraged. Is not the main enemy of a Christian sense of enterprise perhaps a certain functionalism that makes efficiency the one and only and the immediate requirement for production and work?

— TALK IN BARCELONA, SPAIN, NOVEMBER 1982

When a firm makes a profit, this means that productive factors have been properly employed and corresponding human needs have been duly satisfied. But profitability is not the only indicator of a firm's condition. It is possible for the financial accounts to be in order and yet for the people—who make up the firm's most valuable asset—to be humiliated and their dignity offended. Besides being morally inadmissible, this will eventually have negative repercussions on the firm's economic efficiency.

The purpose of a business firm is not simply to make a profit, but is to be found in its very existence as a *community of persons* who in various ways are endeavoring to satisfy their basic needs and who form a particular group at the service of the whole society. Profit is a regulator of the life of a business, but it is not the only one; other human and moral factors must also be considered, which in the long term are at least equally important for the life of a business.

— ENCYCLICAL *CENTESIMUS ANNUS*, MAY 1991

FOR REFLECTION

"It is possible for financial accounts to be in order and yet for human dignity to be offended."

After some study and prayer, a business owner might decide to raise wages in her company—putting her wage scale slightly above her competitors. A CEO might decide to forego some stock options, asking that they be put in a scholarship fund for employees' children.

These are generous gestures. They are not, however, what John Paul II means by social justice in the workplace. Social justice is about improving policies or institutions. For a business leader, it might mean finding other business people who support an increase in the minimum wage. Or it might mean establishing a company policy that caps executives' compensation and proportions it to wages throughout the company.

- Have you ever, in the interest of human dignity, tried to advance a new policy at work, in the community, or even in the home? What happened?

THE GOSPEL OF WORK
IMPLIES A LAY-CENTERED
CHURCH

There is no such thing as *an ordinary lay person*, for all of you have been called to conversion through the death and resurrection of Jesus Christ. As God's holy people you are called to fulfill your role in the evangelization of the world.... It is the specific vocation and mission [of lay people] to express the gospel in their lives and thereby to insert the gospel as a leaven into the reality of the world in which they live and work. The great forces that shape the world—politics, the mass media, science, technology, culture, education, industry, and work—are precisely the areas where lay people are especially competent to exercise their mission. If these forces are guided by people who are true disciples of Christ and who are at the same time fully competent in the relevant secular knowledge and skill, then indeed will the world be transformed from within by Christ's redeeming power.

— HOMILY IN LIMERICK, IRELAND, OCTOBER 1979

It is within the everyday world that you the laity must bear witness to God's kingdom; through you the church's mission is fulfilled by the power of the Holy Spirit. The [Second Vatican] Council taught that the specific task of the laity is precisely this: To "seek the kingdom of God by engaging in temporal affairs and by ordering them according to the plan of God."

You are called to live in the world, to engage in secular professions and occupations, to live in those ordinary circumstances of family life and life in society from which is woven the very web of your existence. You are called by God…to work for the sanctification of the world from within, in the manner of leaven….

Every age poses new challenges and new temptations for the people of God on their pilgrimage, and our own is no exception. We face a growing secularism that tries to exclude God and religious truth from human affairs. We face an insidious relativism that undermines the absolute truth of Christ and the truths of faith, and tempts believers to think of them as merely one set of beliefs or opinions among others. We face a materialistic consumerism that offers superficially attractive but empty promises conferring material comfort at the price of inner emptiness. We face an alluring hedonism that offers a whole series of pleasures that will never satisfy the human heart….

It is precisely in this society that lay men and women like yourselves, all the Catholic laity, are called to live the Beatitudes, to become leaven, salt, and light for the world, and sometimes a sign of contradiction that challenges and transforms the world according to the mind of Christ. No one is called to impose religious beliefs on others, but to give the strong example of a life of justice and service, resplendent with virtues of faith, hope, and charity….

The greatest challenge to the conscience of society comes from your fidelity to your own Christian vocation. It is up to you the Catholic laity to incarnate without ceasing the gospel in society—in American society.

— Talk in San Francisco, United States, September 1987

The eyes of faith behold a wonderful scene: that of a countless number of lay people, both women and men, busy at

31

work in their daily life and activity, oftentimes far from view and quite overlooked by the world, unknown to the world's great personages but nonetheless looked upon in love by the Father, untiring laborers who work in the Lord's vineyard. Confident and steadfast through the power of God's grace, these are the humble yet great builders of the kingdom of God in history....

The lay faithful are never to relinquish their participation in public life, that is, in the many different economic, social, legislative, administrative, and cultural areas, which are intended to promote organically and institutionally the common good....There cannot be two parallel lives in [a lay person's] existence: on the one hand, the so-called *spiritual life*, with its values and demands; and on the other, the so-called *secular life* in family, at work, in social relationships, in the responsibilities of public life, and in culture....In fact, every area of the laity's lives, as different as they are, enters into the plan of God, who desires that these very areas be the places in time where the love of Christ is revealed and realized for both the glory of the Father and service of others. Every activity, every situation, every precise responsibility—as, for example, skill and solidarity in work, love and dedication in the family and the education of children, service to society and public life, and the promotion of truth in the area of culture—are the occasions ordained by providence for a continuous exercise of faith, hope, and charity....

[As Pope] Pius XII once stated: [the laity] ought to have an ever-clearer consciousness not only of belonging to the church, but of being the church....The lay faithful are the church.

— APOSTOLIC EXHORTATION *CHRISTIFIDELES LAICI*, JANUARY 1989

FOR REFLECTION

"Sanctify the world from within, like leaven."

A central theme of John Paul II's travels around the world was the insistence that lay people are the church and that they have a duty to humanize their cities, countries, and cultures by working from within their normal settings. The best apostles are those closest to the situation.

- Name an apostolic situation from the previous week at your place of work, your office, your neighborhood, or your home? Did you succeed or did you fail?

- John Paul II urges us to spread our faith and yet not to impose our religious beliefs on others. Have you recently had a true dialog with someone about faith or morality? Do you ever discuss faith or morality with non-Christian friends or colleagues? Why or why not?

On Human Work (*Laborem Exercens*)

ENCYCLICAL OF POPE JOHN PAUL II
(SEPTEMBER 14, 1981)

The encyclical that follows doesn't "solve" anything. It is instead visionary. It is more meditative and less directive than some papal documents. (It is therefore somewhat repetitious.)

Laborem Exercens is John Paul II's invitation to think out loud about the implications of a business, an economy, indeed, a civilization based on meaningful work. Before you begin reading it, consider the following.

- Many businesses occasionally and even routinely have staff retreats, visioning sessions, and mission statement reviews. What has been your experience with in-service days and other reflection sessions at your place of employment?

- Is there a forum in which from time to time you can discuss the meaning of work? Is that topic a component of your annual employee review? If it isn't should it be?

- Could your parish sponsor a monthly breakfast or an annual retreat on the meaning of work?

Venerable Brothers and Dear Sons and Daughters, Greetings and the Apostolic Blessing.

Through work people must earn their daily bread[1] and contribute to the continual advance of science and technology and, above all, to elevating unceasingly the cultural and moral level of the society within which we live in community with those who belong to the same family. And work means any activity, whether manual or intellectual, whatever its nature or circumstances; it means any human activity that can and must be recognized as work, in the midst of all the many activities of which people are capable and predisposed by their very nature, by virtue of humanity itself. People are made to be in the visible universe and image and likeness of God,[2] and placed in it in order to subdue the earth.³ From the beginning therefore people are called to work. Work is one of the characteristics that distinguish humans from the rest of creatures, whose activity for sustaining their lives cannot be called work. Only humans are capable of work, and only people work, at the same time by work occupying existence on earth. Thus work bears a particular mark of humanity, the mark of a person operating within a community of persons. And this mark decides its interior characteristics; in a sense it constitutes its very nature.

I. INTRODUCTION

Human Work on the Ninetieth Anniversary of *Rerum Novarum*

Since May 15, 1981 was the ninetieth anniversary of the publication by the great pope of the "social question," Pope Leo XIII, of the decisively important encyclical which begins with the words *Rerum novarum*, I wish to devote this document to human work and, even more, to people in the vast context of the reality of work. As I said in the encyclical *Redemptor Hominis*, published at the beginning of my service in the See of Saint Peter in Rome, humankind "is the primary and fundamental way for the Church,"⁴ precisely because of the inscrutable mystery of redemption in Christ; and so it is necessary to return constantly to this way and to follow it ever anew in the various aspects in which it shows us all the wealth and at the same time all the toil of human existence on earth.

Work is one of these aspects, a perennial and fundamental one, one that is always relevant and constantly demands renewed attention and decisive witness. Because fresh questions and problems are always arising, there are always fresh hopes, but also fresh fears and threats, connected with this basic dimension of human existence: human life is built up every day from work, from work it derives its specific dignity, but at the same time work contains the unceasing measure of human toil and suffering, and also of the harm and injustice which penetrate deeply into social life within individual nations and on the international level. While it is true that people eat the bread produced by the work of human hands[5]—and this means not only the daily bread by which the body keeps alive but also the bread of science and progress, civilization and culture—it is also a perennial truth that people eat this bread by "the sweat of his brow,"[6] that is to say, not only by personal effort and toil but also in the midst of many tensions, conflicts, and crises, which, in relationship with the reality of work, disturb the life of individual societies and also of all humanity.

We are celebrating the ninetieth anniversary of the encyclical *Rerum Novarum* on the eve of new developments in technological, economic, and political conditions that, according to many experts, will influence the world of work and production no less than the industrial revolution of the last century. There are many factors of a general nature: the widespread introduction of automation into many spheres of production; the increase in the cost of energy and raw materials; the growing realization that the heritage of nature is limited and that it is being intolerably polluted; and the emergence on the political scene of people who, after centuries of subjection, are demanding their rightful place among the nations and in international decision-making. These new conditions and demands will require a reordering and adjustment of the structures of the modern economy and of the distribution of work. Unfortunately, for millions of skilled workers these changes may perhaps mean unemployment, at least for a time, or the need for retraining. They will very probably involve a reduction or a less rapid increase in material well-being for the more developed countries. But they can also bring relief and hope to the millions who today live in conditions of shameful and unworthy poverty.

It is not for the church to analyze scientifically the consequences that these changes may have on human society. But the church considers it her task always to call attention to the dignity and rights of those who work, to condemn situations in which that dignity and those rights are violated, and to help to guide the above mentioned changes so as to ensure authentic progress by people and society.

In the Organic Development of the Church's Social Action

It is certainly true that work, as a human issue, is at the very center of the "social question" to which, for almost a hundred years, since the publication of the above-mentioned encyclical, the church's teaching and the many undertakings connected with her apostolic mission have been especially directed. The present reflections on work are not intended to follow a different line, but rather to be in organic connection with the whole tradition of this teaching and activity. At the same time, however, I am making them, according to the indication in the gospel, in order to bring out from the heritage of the gospel "what is new and what is old."[7] Certainly, work is part of "what is old"—as old as human life on earth. Nevertheless, the general situation in the modern world, studied and analyzed in its various aspects of geography, culture, and civilization, calls for the discovery of the new meanings of human work. It likewise calls for the formulation of the new tasks that in this sector face each individual, the family, each country, the whole human race, and, finally, the church herself.

During the years that separate us from the publication of the encyclical *Rerum Novarum*, the social question has not ceased to engage the church's attention. Evidence of this are the many documents of the magisterium issued by the popes and by the Second Vatican Council, pronouncements by individual episcopates, and the activity of the various centers of thought and of practical apostolic initiatives, both on the international level and at the level of the local churches. It is difficult to list here in detail all the manifestations of the commitment of the church and of Christians in the social question, for they are too numerous. As a result of the Council, the main coordinating center in this field is the Pontifical Commission Justice and Peace, which has corresponding bodies within the individual Bishops' Conferences. The name of this institution is very significant. It indicates that the social question must be dealt with in its whole complex dimension. Commitment to justice must be closely linked with commitment to peace in the modern world. This twofold commitment is certainly supported by the painful experience of the two great world wars that in the course of the last ninety years have convulsed many European countries and, at least partially, countries in other continents. It is supported especially since World War II, by the permanent threat of a nuclear war and the prospect of the terrible self-destruction that emerges from it.

If we follow the main line of development of the documents of the supreme magisterium of the church, we find in them an explicit confirmation of precisely such a statement of the question. The key position, as regards the question of world peace, is that of John XXIII's encyclical *Pacem in Terris*. However, if one studies the development of the question of social justice, one cannot fail to note that, whereas during the period between *Rerum Novarum* and Pius XI's *Quadragesimo Anno*, the church's teaching concentrates mainly on the just solution of the "labor question" within individual nations, in the next period the church's teaching widens its horizon to take in the whole world. The disproportionate distribution of wealth and poverty and the existence of some countries and continents that are developed and of others that are not, call for a leveling out and for a search for ways to ensure just development for all. This is the direction of the teaching in John XXIII's encyclical *Mater et Magistra*, in the Pastoral Constitution *Gaudium et Spes* of the Second Vatican Council, and in Paul VI's encyclical *Populorum Progressio*.

This trend of development of the church's teaching and commitment in the social question exactly corresponds to the objective recognition of the state of affairs. While in the past the "class" question was especially highlighted as the center of this issue, in more recent times it is the "world" question that is emphasized. Thus, not only the sphere of class is taken into consideration but also the world sphere of inequality and injustice, and as a consequence, not only the class dimension but also the world dimension of the tasks involved in the path toward the achievement of justice in the modern world. A complete analysis of the situation of the world today shows in an even deeper and fuller way the meaning of the previous analysis of social injustices; and it is the meaning that must be given today to efforts to build justice on earth, not concealing thereby unjust structures but demanding that they be examined and transformed on a more universal scale.

FOR REFLECTION

If we get work right, John Paul II seems to say, we get everything right.

Work done with competence in well-organized workplaces and within a just marketplace will have many beneficial effects. Family life will all the more reflect the love of God when parents come home from a meaningful job (be it a job outdoors, in a downtown office, in a medical facility, or in a factory), a job that pays a just wage or salary. Poverty will best be diminished by creating living wage jobs for all who are capable. Education will proceed as smoothly as possible when students and their teachers know that their aspirations find challenging outlets in the marketplace of ideas, products, and relationships. Defects in the culture, including abortion and euthanasia, will best be addressed when workers have the capacity to see the innate dignity of their co-workers, their patients, their suppliers, their clients, their students, their managers, and all the people they encounter all week long.

Where to start in an effort to have a better family, a better neighborhood, a better society, and a better world? The issues and the dynamics seem overwhelming. John Paul II suggests we start at and end with work. Want a better world? Try to

The Question of Work, the Key to the Social Question

In the midst of all these processes—those of the diagnosis of objective social reality and also those of the church's teaching in the sphere of the complex and many-sided social question—the question of human work naturally appears many times. This issue is, in a way, a constant factor both of social life and of the church's teaching. Furthermore, in this teaching attention to the question goes back much further than the last ninety years. In fact, the church's social teaching finds its source in sacred scripture, beginning with the Book of Genesis and especially

construct a civilization based on good work.

For insights into the nature and meaning of work, John Paul II turns to his favorite book in the Bible, Genesis.

The earth, says Genesis, was a "formless void" before God began to work. Some translations say it was "formless and desolate," or more accurately, it was "total chaos." During the first days of work God was busy separating this from that, putting the light here and the darkness there.

The whole notion of making a home out of the earth has to do with order. People are at home, God knows, when their surroundings are sufficiently predictable to afford safety and purpose. Sin is the disruption of God's plan for the ideal home. Sin makes the world less predictable, less safe, and more chaotic, out of harmony with its divine purpose.

- Until we experience our world as a reliable place, says psychologist Eric Erickson, personal development is impossible. What institutions, in your opinion, routinely make our world a safe home, a better place to live?

- How does your work contribute to patterns of safety or to harmony?

in the gospel and the writings of the apostles. From the beginning it was part of the church's teaching, her concept of humankind and life in society, and especially the social morality which she worked out according to the needs of the different ages. This traditional patrimony was then inherited and developed by the teaching of the popes on the modern "social question," beginning with the encyclical *Rerum Novarum*. In this context, study of the question of work, as we have seen, has continually been brought up to date while maintaining that Christian basis of truth which can be called ageless.

While in the present document we return to this question once more—without however any intention of touching on all the topics that concern it—this it not merely in order to gather together and repeat what is already contained in the church's teaching. It is rather in order to highlight—perhaps more than has been done before—the fact that human work is a key, probably the essential key, to the whole social question, if we try to see that question really from the point of view of goodness. And if the solution—or rather the gradual solution—of the social question, which keeps coming up and becomes ever more complex, must be sought in the direction of "making life more human,"[8] then the key, namely human work, acquires fundamental and decisive importance.

II. WORK AND HUMANKIND

In the Book of Genesis

The church is convinced that work is a fundamental dimension of human existence on earth. She is confirmed in this conviction by considering the whole heritage of the many sciences: anthropology, paleontology, history, sociology, psychology, and so on; they all seem to bear witness to this reality in an irrefutable way. But the source of the church's conviction is above all the revealed word of God, and therefore what is a conviction of the intellect is also a conviction of faith. The reason is that the church—and it is worthwhile stating it at this point—believes in people: she thinks of humankind and addresses herself to people not only in the light of historical experience, not only with the aid of the many methods of scientific knowledge, but in the first place in the light of the revealed word of the living God. Relating herself to people, she seeks to express the eternal designs and transcendent destiny of the living God, the Creator and Redeemer.

The church finds in the very first pages of the Book of Genesis the source of her conviction that work is a fundamental dimension of human existence on earth. An analysis of these texts makes us aware that they express—sometimes in an archaic way of manifesting thought—the fundamental truths about humankind, in the context of the mystery of creation itself. These truths are decisive from the very beginning, and at the same time they trace out the main lines of earthly existence, both in the state of original justice and also after the breaking, caused by sin, of the Creator's original covenant with creation in man. When people, who had been created "in the image of God…male and female,"[9] hear the words: "Be fruitful and multiply, and fill the earth and subdue it,"[10] even though these words do not refer directly and explicitly to work, beyond any doubt they indirectly indicate it as an activity for people to carry out in the world. Indeed, they show its very deepest essence. People are the image of God partly through the mandate received from the Creator to subdue, to dominate, the earth. In carrying out this mandate, every human being reflects the very action of the Creator of the universe.

Work understood as a "transitive" activity, that is to say an activity beginning in the human subject and directed toward an external object, presupposes a specific dominion by humankind over "the earth," and in its turn it confirms and develops this dominion. It is clear that the term "the earth," of which the biblical text speaks, is to be understood in the first place as that fragment of the visible universe that people inhabit. By extension, however, it can be understood as the whole of the visible world insofar as it comes within the range of human influence and of the striving to satisfy human needs. The expression "subdue the earth" has an immense range. It means all the resources that the earth (and indirectly the visible world) contains and which, through conscious activity, can be discovered and used for human ends. And so these words, placed at the beginning of the Bible, never cease to be relevant. They embrace equally the past ages of civilization and economy, as also the whole of modern reality and future phases of development, which are perhaps already to some extent beginning to take shape, though for the most part they are still almost unknown to and hidden from people.

While people sometimes speak of periods of "acceleration" in the economic life and civilization of humanity or of individual nations, linking these periods to the progress of science and technology and especially to discoveries which are decisive for social and economic life, at the same time it can be said that none of these phenomena of "acceleration" exceeds the essential content of what was said in that most ancient of biblical texts. As people, through work, become more and more the master of the earth, and as they confirm dominion over the visible world, again through work, they nevertheless remain in every case and at every phase of this process within the Creator's original ordering. And this ordering remains necessarily and indissolubly linked with the fact that humankind was created, as male and female, "in the image of God." This process is, at the same time, universal: It embraces all human beings, every generation, every phase of economic and cultural development, and at the same time it is a process that takes place within each human being, in each conscious human being, in each conscious human subject. Each and every individual is at the same time embraced by it. Each and every individual, to the proper extent and in an incalculable number of ways, takes part in the giant process whereby man "subdues the earth" through work.

Work in the Objective Sense: Technology

This universality and, at the same time, this multiplicity of the process of "subduing the earth" throws light upon human work, because dominion over the earth is achieved in and by means of work. There thus emerges the meaning of work in an objective sense, which finds expression in the various epochs of culture and civilization. People dominate the earth by the very fact of domesticating animals, rearing them and obtaining from them needed food and clothing, and by the fact of being able to extract various natural resources from the earth and the seas. But people "subdue the earth" much more when they begin to cultivate it and then to transform its products, adapting them to their use. Thus agriculture constitutes through human work a primary field of economic activity and an indispensable factor of production. Industry in its turn will always consist in linking the earth's riches—whether nature's living resources, or the products of agriculture, or the mineral or chemical resources—with work, whether physical or intellectual. This is also in a sense true in the sphere of what are called service industries, and also in the sphere of research, pure or applied.

In industry and agriculture work has today in many cases ceased to be mainly manual, for the toil of human hands and muscles is aided by more and more highly perfected machinery. Not only in industry but also in agriculture we are witnessing the transformations made possible by the gradual development of science and technology. Historically speaking, this, taken as a whole, has caused great changes in civilization, from the beginning of the "industrial era" to the successive phases of development through new technologies, such as electronics and the microprocessor technology in recent years.

While it may seem that in the industrial process it is the machine that "works" and people merely supervise it, make it function, and keep it going in various ways, it is also true that for this very reason industrial development provides grounds for proposing in new ways the question of human work. Both the original industrialization that gave rise to what is called the worker question and the subsequent industrial and post-industrial changes show in an eloquent manner that, even in the age of ever more mechanized "work," the proper subject of work continues to be humankind.

The development of industry and of the various sectors connected with it, even the most modern electronics technology, especially in the fields of miniaturization, communications and telecommunications, and so forth, show how vast is the role of technology, that ally of work that human thought has produced, in the interaction between the subject and object of work (in the widest sense of the word). Understood in this case not as a capacity or aptitude for work, but rather as a whole set of instruments which people use in work, technology is undoubtedly our ally. It facilitates work, perfects, accelerates, and augments it. It leads to an increase in the quantity of things produced by work, and, in many cases, improves their quality. However, it is also a fact that in some instances technology can cease to be an ally and become almost an enemy, as when the mechanization of work "supplants" people, taking away all personal satisfaction and the incentive to creativity and responsibility, when it deprives many workers of their previous employment, or when, through exalting the machine, it reduces people to the status of its slave.

If the biblical words "subdue the earth" addressed to people from the very beginning are understood in the context of the whole modern age, industrial and post-industrial, then they undoubtedly include also a relationship with technology, with the world of machinery which is the fruit of the work of the human intellect and a historical confirmation of dominion over nature.

The recent stage of human history, especially that of certain societies, brings a correct affirmation of technology as a basic coefficient of economic progress; but at the same time this affirmation has been accompanied by and continues to be accompanied by essential questions concerning human work in relationship to its subject, which is humankind. These questions are particularly charged with content and

48

tension of an ethical and social character. They therefore constitute a continual challenge for institutions of many kinds, for states and governments, for systems and international organizations; they also constitute a challenge for the church.

FOR REFLECTION

This encyclical is an example of creation-centered theology. But John Paul II does not confine creativity to the arts, although he appreciates them. According to John Paul II all, workers are artists.

We are images of God not only because we can reason and exercise free will, but also because we work. Our creation, he insists, includes boilers, highways, computer programs, and all of our technology.

Here and elsewhere John Paul II implies at least that the fruit of human work, our technology, is in some sense creating heaven.

- Have you ever considered yourself, especially at work, as an image of God? Why or why not?

Work in the Subjective Sense: People as the Subject of Work

In order to continue our analysis of work, an analysis linked with the word of the Bible telling people that they are to subdue the earth, we must concentrate our attention on work in the subjective sense, much more than we did on the objective significance, barely touching upon the vast range of problems known intimately and in detail to scholars in various fields and also, according to their specializations, to those who work. If the words of the Book of Genesis to which I refer in this analysis of ours speak of work in the objective sense in an indirect way, they also speak only indirectly of the subject of work; but what they say is very eloquent and is full of great significance.

People have to subdue the earth and dominate it, because as the "image of God" they are subjective beings capable of acting in a planned and rational way, capable of deciding and with a tendency to self-realization. As a person, people are therefore the subject of work. As a person they work, they perform various actions belonging to the work process; independently of their objective content, these actions must all serve to realize humanity, to fulfill the calling to be a person that is by the very reason of humanity. The principal truths concerning this theme were recently recalled by the Second Vatican Council in the constitution *Gaudium et Spes*, especially in Chapter One, which is devoted to people's calling.

And so this "dominion" spoken of in the biblical text being meditated upon here refers not only to the objective dimension of work, but at the same time introduces us to an understanding of its subjective dimension. Understood as a process whereby the human race subdues the earth, work corresponds to this basic biblical concept only when throughout the process the worker manifests and confirms people as the ones who "dominate." This dominion, in a certain sense, refers to the subjective dimension even more than to the objective one: this dimension conditions the very ethical nature of work. In fact there is no doubt that human work has an ethical value of its own, which clearly and directly remains linked to the fact that the one who carries it out is a person, a conscious and free subject, that is to say, a subject that decides about himself [or herself].

This truth, which in a sense constitutes the fundamental and perennial heart of Christian teaching on human work, has had and continues to have primary significance for the formulation of the important social problems characterizing whole ages.

The ancient world introduced its own typical differentiation of people into classes according to the type of work done. Work which demanded from the worker the exercise of physical strength, the work of muscles and hands, was considered unworthy of free men and was therefore given to slaves. By broadening certain aspects that already belonged to the Old Testament, Christianity brought about a fundamental change of ideas in this field, taking the whole content of the gospel message as its point of departure, especially the fact that the one who, while being God, became like us in all things,[11] devoting most of the years of his life on earth to manual work at the carpenter's bench. This circumstance constitutes in itself the most eloquent "gospel of work," showing that the basis for determining the value of human work is not primarily the kind of work being done, but the fact that the one who is doing it is a person. The sources of the dignity of work are to be sought primarily in the subjective dimension, not in the objective one.

Such a concept practically does away with the very basis of the ancient differentiation of people into classes according to the kind of work done. This does not mean that from the objective point of view human work cannot and must not be rated and qualified in any way. It only means that the primary basis of the value of work is a human being, who is its subject. This leads immediately to a very important conclusion of an ethical nature: however true it may be that people are destined for work and called to it, in the first place work is "for people" and not people "for work." Through this conclusion one rightly comes to recognize the pre-eminence of the subjective meaning of work over the objective one. Given this way of understanding things and presupposing that different sorts of work that people do can have greater or lesser objective value, let us try nevertheless to show that each sort is judged above all by the measure of the dignity of the subject of work, that is to say, the person, the individual who carries it out. On the other hand, independent of the work that every person does, and presupposing that this work constitutes a purpose—at times a very demanding one—of activity, this purpose does not possess a definitive meaning in itself. In fact, in the final analysis it is always the person who is the purpose of the work, whatever work it is that is done—even if the common scale of values rates it as the merest "service," as the most monotonous, even the most alienating work.

FOR REFLECTION

Here and in several other places in this encyclical, John Paul II states his major theme: all work has dignity (equal dignity) because the work is done by a human being.

Of course a budget manager or an accountant must have a line on his or her reports called "salaries and wages." Of course a financial vice-president must think about "payroll" in somewhat impersonal or general terms. Of course business students must learn how to calculate the labor costs in a business. But, John Paul II insists, labor is not just one more "cost of doing business." It is not a raw material. Nor should workers think of their labor as merchandise they sell to an employer.

The whole purpose of a business and of an economy is to afford people the opportunity to bring their talents to the marketplace and to reward those talents in such a way that workers can feed and educate their families. If we get work right, we get everything right.

- "The value of work comes not from the job title but from the fact that the work is done by a person." How do you react to this statement?

- How would things change if a sign about the equal dignity of work was prominently displayed at your business? How would the relations between nurses and doctors, between pastors and grammar school teachers, between professors and secretaries change?

- Why do many businesses have reserved parking spaces for executives? By contrast, are there policies at your workplace that strive to make all workers feel included in the business?

A Threat to the Right Order of Values

It is precisely these fundamental affirmations about work that always emerged from the wealth of Christian truth, especially from the very message of the "gospel of work," thus creating the basis for a new way of thinking, judging, and acting. In the modern period, from the beginning of the industrial age, the Christian truth about work had to oppose the various trends of materialistic and economistic thought.

For certain supporters of such ideas, work was understood and treated as a sort of "merchandise" that the worker—especially the industrial worker—sells to the employer, who at the same time is the possessor of the capital, that is to say, of all the working tools and means that make production possible. This way of looking at work was widespread especially in the first half of the nineteenth century. Since then explicit expressions of this sort have almost disappeared and have given way to more human ways of thinking about work and evaluating it. The interaction between the worker and the tools and means of production has given rise to the development of various forms of capitalism—parallel with various forms of collectivism—into which other socioeconomic elements have entered as a consequence of new concrete circumstances, of the activity of workers' associations and public authorities, and of the emergence of large transnational enterprises. Nevertheless, the danger of treating work as a special kind of "merchandise" or as an impersonal "force" needed for production (the expression "workforce" is in fact in common use) always exists, especially when the whole way of looking at the question of economics is marked by the premises of materialistic economism.

A systematic opportunity for thinking and evaluating in this way, and in a certain sense a stimulus for doing so, is provided by the quickening process of the development of a one-sidedly materialistic civilization, which gives prime importance to the objective dimension of work, while the subjective dimension—everything in direct or indirect relationship with the subject of work—remains on a secondary level. In all cases of this sort, in every social situation of this type, there is a confusion or even a reversal of the order laid down from the beginning by the words of the Book of Genesis: People are treated as an instrument of production,[12] whereas people—alone, independent of the work they do—ought to be treated as the effective subject of work and its true maker and creator. Precisely this reversal of order, whatever the program or name under which it occurs, should rightly be called "capitalism"—in the sense more fully explained below. Everybody knows that capitalism has a definite historical meaning as a system, an economic and social system, opposed to "socialism" or "communism." But in light of the analysis of the fundamental reality of the whole economic process—first and foremost of the production structure that work is—it should be recognized that the error of early capitalism can be repeated wherever people are in a way treated on the same level as the whole complex of the material means of production, as an instrument and not in accordance with the true dignity of their work—that is to say, where people are not treated as subject and maker, and for this very reason as the true purpose of the whole process of production.

This explains why the analysis of human work in the light of the works concerning people's "dominion" over the earth goes to the very heart of the ethical and social question. This concept should also find a central place in the whole sphere of social and economic policy, both within individual countries and in the wider field of international and intercontinental relationships, particularly with reference to the tensions making themselves felt in the world not only between East and West but also between North and South. Both John XXIII in the encyclical *Mater et Magistra* and Paul VI in the encyclical *Populorum Progressio* gave special attention to these dimensions of the modern ethical and social question.

Worker Solidarity

When dealing with human work in the fundamental dimension of its subject, that is to say, the human person doing work, one must make at least a summary evaluation of developments during the ninety years since *Rerum Novarum* in relation to the subjective dimension of work. Although the subject of work is always the same, that is to say humankind, nevertheless wide-ranging changes take place in the objective aspect. While one can say that, by reason of its subject, work is one single thing (one and unrepeatable every time) yet when one takes into consideration its objective directions one is forced to admit that there exist many works, many different sorts of work. The development of human civilization brings continual enrichment in this field. But at the same time, one cannot fail to note that in the process of this development not only do new forms of work appear but also others disappear. Even if one accepts that on the whole this is a normal phenomenon, it must still be seen whether certain ethically and socially dangerous irregularities creep in and to what extent.

It was precisely one such wide-ranging anomaly that gave rise in the last century to what has been called "the worker question," sometimes described as "the proletariat question." This question and the problems connected with it gave rise to a just social reaction and caused the impetuous emergence of a great burst of solidarity between workers, first and foremost industrial workers. The call to solidarity and common action addressed to the workers—especially to those engaged in narrowly specialized, monotonous, and depersonalized work in industrial plants, when the machine tends to dominate people—was important and eloquent from the point of view of social ethics. It was the reaction against the degradation of humans as the subject of work and against the unheard of accompanying exploitation in the field of wages, working conditions, and social security for the worker. This reaction united the working world in a community marked by great solidarity.

Following the lines laid down by the encyclical *Rerum Novarum* and many later documents of the church's magisterium, it must be frankly recognized that the reaction against the system of injustice and harm that cried to heaven for vengeance[13] and that weighed heavily upon workers in that period of rapid industrialization was justified from the point of view of social morality. This state of affairs was favored by the liberal sociopolitical system, which in accordance with its "economistic" premises, strengthened and safeguarded economic initiative by the possessors of capital alone, but did not pay sufficient attention to the rights of the workers, on the grounds that human work is solely an instrument of production, and that capital is the basis, efficient factor and purpose of production.

FOR REFLECTION

In Catholic social thought the term "social justice" is used more precisely than in common political commentary. The unique act of social justice, says Catholic philosophy, is organizing like-minded people to improve policies or institutions.

There is, admittedly, a constant need for prophetic or outsider critiques of society, but that is not the primary way of social justice. Mainstream Catholic experience finds that the virtue of social justice is normally exercised within one's own workplace or community or family setting.

- How can you, along with like-minded colleagues, use your job or your position in the community as a vehicle for social change?

- Is work life and its potential for justice ever discussed at your parish or school? In what ways? What might you do to get these discussions started?

From that time, worker solidarity, together with a clearer and more committed realization by others of workers' rights, has in many cases brought about profound changes. Various forms of neo-capitalism or collectivism have developed. Various new systems have been thought out. Workers can often share in running businesses and in controlling their productivity, and in fact do so. Through appropriate associations they exercise influence over conditions of work and pay and also over social legislation. But at the same time various ideological or power systems and new relationships that have arisen at various levels of society have allowed flagrant injustices to persist or have created new ones. On the world level, the development of civilization and of communications has made possible a more complete diagnosis of the living and working conditions globally, but it has also revealed other forms of injustice much more extensive than those which in the last century stimulated unity between workers for particular solidarity in the working world. This is true in countries that have completed a certain process of industrial revolution. It is also true in countries where the main working milieu continues to be agriculture or other similar occupations.

Movements of solidarity in the sphere of work—a solidarity that must never mean being closed to dialogue and collaboration with others—can be necessary also with reference to the condition of social groups that were not previously included in such movements, but which in changing social systems and conditions of living are undergoing what is in effect "proletarianization" or which actually already find themselves in a "proletariat" situation, one which, even if not yet given that name, in fact deserves it. This can be true of certain categories or groups of the working "intelligentsia," especially whenever wider access to education and an ever-increasing number of people with degrees or diplomas in the fields of their cultural preparation are accompanied by a drop in demand for their labor. This unemployment of intellectuals occurs or increases when the education available is not oriented toward the types of employment or service required by the true needs of society, or when there is less demand for work which requires education, at least professional education, than for manual labor, or when it is less well paid. Of course, education in itself is always valuable and an important enrichment of the human person; but in spite of that "proletarianization" processes remain possible.

For this reason, there must be continued study of the subject of work and of the subject's living conditions. In order to achieve social justice in the various parts of the world, in the various countries and in the relationships between them, there is a need for ever new movements of solidarity of the workers and with the workers. This solidarity must be present whenever it is called for by the social degrading of the subject of work, by exploitation of the workers, and by the growing areas of poverty and even hunger. The church is firmly committed to this cause for she considers it her mission, her service, a proof of her fidelity to Christ, so that she can truly be the "church of the poor." And the "poor" appear under various forms; they appear in various places and at various times; in many cases they appear as a result of the violation of the dignity of human work: either because the opportunities for human work are limited as a result of the scourge of unemployment, or because a low value is put on work and the rights that flow from it, especially the right to a just wage and to the personal security of the worker and his or her family.

Work and Personal Dignity

Remaining within the context of people as the subject of work, it is now appropriate to touch upon, at least in a summary way, certain problems that more closely define the dignity of human work in that they make it possible to characterize more fully its specific moral value. In doing this we must always keep in mind the biblical calling to "subdue the earth,"[14] in which is expressed the will of the Creator that work should enable people to achieve that "dominion" in the visible world that is proper to humankind.

God's fundamental and original intention with regard to people, whom God created in his image and after his likeness,[15] was not withdrawn or canceled out even when people, having broken the original covenant with God, heard the words: "In the sweat of your face you shall eat bread."[16] These words refer to the sometimes heavy toil that from then onward has accompanied human work; but they do not alter the fact that work is the means whereby people achieve that "dominion" which is proper over the visible world, by "subjecting" the earth. Toil is something that is universally known, for it is universally experienced. It is familiar to those doing physical work under sometimes exceptionally laborious conditions. It is familiar not only to agricultural workers, who spend long days working the land, which sometimes "bears thorns and thistles,"[17] but also to those who work in mines and quarries, to steelworkers at their blast furnaces, to those who work in builders' yards and in construction work, often in danger of injury or death. It is also familiar to those at an intellectual workbench; to scientists; to those who bear the burden of grave responsibility for decisions that will have a vast impact on society. It is familiar to doctors and nurses, who spend days and nights at their patients' bedside. It is familiar to women, who sometimes without proper recognition on the part of society and even of their own families, bear the daily burden and responsibility for their homes and the upbringing of their children. It is familiar to all workers and, since work is a universal calling it is familiar to everyone.

And yet in spite of all this toil—perhaps, in a sense, because of it—work is a good thing for people. Even though it bears the mark of a *bonum arduum*, in the terminology of St. Thomas,[18] this does not take away the fact that, as such, it is a good thing. It is not only good in the sense that it is useful or something to enjoy, it is also good as being something worthy, that is to say, something that corresponds to human dignity, that expresses this dignity and increases it. If one wishes to define more clearly the ethical meaning of work, it is this truth that one must particularly keep in mind. Work is a good thing for people—a good thing for their humanity—because through work people not only transform nature, adapting it to their own needs, but they also achieve fulfillment as a human being and indeed in a sense become "more a human being."

Without this consideration it is impossible to understand the meaning of the virtue of industriousness, and more particularly it is impossible to understand why industriousness should be a virtue: For virtue, as a moral habit, is something whereby people become good as people.[19] This fact in no way alters our justifiable anxiety that in work, whereby matter gains in nobility, a person should not experience a lowering of their own dignity.[20] Again, it is well known that it is possible to use work in various ways against a person, that it is possible to punish people with the system of forced labor in concentration camps, that work can be made into a means for oppressing people, and that in various ways it is possible to exploit human labor, that is to say, the worker. All this pleads in favor of the moral obligation to link industriousness as a virtue with the social order of work, which will enable people to become in work "more a human being" and not be degraded by it, not only because of the wearing out of physical strength (which, at least up to a certain point, is inevitable), but especially through damage to the dignity and subjectivity that are proper to humankind.

Work and Society: Family and Nation

Having thus confirmed the personal dimension of human work, I must go on to the second sphere of values, which is necessarily linked to work. Work constitutes a foundation for the formation of family life, which is a natural right and something that people are called to. These two spheres of values—one linked to work and the other consequent on the family nature of human life—must be properly united and must properly permeate each other. In a way, work is a condition for making it possible to found a family, since the family requires the means of subsistence which people normally gain through work. Work and

60

industriousness also influence the whole process of education in the family, for the very reason that everyone "becomes a human being" through, among other things, work, and becoming a human being is precisely the main purpose of the whole process of education. Obviously, two aspects of work in a sense come into play here: the one making family life and its upkeep possible, and the other making possible the achievement of the purposes of the family, especially education. Nevertheless, these two aspects of work are linked to one another and are mutually complementary in various points.

It must be remembered and affirmed that the family constitutes one of the most important terms of reference for shaping the social and ethical order of human work. The teaching of the church has always devoted special attention to this question, and in the present document I shall have to return to it. In fact, the family is simultaneously a community made possible by work and the first school of work, within the home, for every person.

The third sphere of values that emerges from this point of view—that of the subject of work—concerns the great society to which people belong on the basis of particular cultural and historical links. This society—even when it has not yet taken on the mature form of a nation—is not only the great "educator" of every person, even though an indirect one (because each individual absorbs within the family the contents and values that go to make up the culture of a given nation); it is also a great historical and social incarnation of the work of all generations. All of this brings it about that people combine their deepest human identity with membership of a nation, and intend work also to increase the common good developed together with compatriots, thus realizing that in this way work serves to add to the heritage of the whole human family, of all the people living in the world.

These three spheres are always important for human work in its subjective dimension. And this dimension, that is to say, the concrete reality of the worker, takes precedence over the objective dimension. In the subjective dimension there is realized, first of all, that "dominion" over the world of nature to which people are called from the beginning according to the words of the Book of Genesis. The very process of "subduing the earth," that is to say work, is marked in the course of history and especially in recent centuries by an immense development of technological means. This is an advantageous and positive phenomenon, on condition that the objective dimension of work does not gain the upper hand over the subjective dimension, depriving man of his dignity and inalienable rights or reducing them.

III. CONFLICT BETWEEN LABOR AND CAPITAL IN THE PRESENT PHASE OF HISTORY

Dimensions of the Conflict

The sketch of the basic problems of work outlined above draws inspiration from the texts at the beginning of the Bible and in a sense forms the very framework of the church's teaching, which has remained unchanged throughout the centuries within the context of different historical experiences. However, the experiences preceding and following the publication of the encyclical *Rerum Novarum* form a background that endows that teaching with particular expressiveness and the eloquence of living relevance. In this analysis, work is seen as a great reality with a fundamental influence on the shaping in a human way of the world that the Creator has entrusted to people; it is a reality closely linked with people as the subjects of work and with rational activity. In the normal course of events this reality fills human life and strongly affects its value and meaning. Even when it is accompanied by toil and effort, work is still something good, and so people develop through love for work. This entirely positive and creative, educational and meritorious character of work must be the basis for the judgments and decisions being made today in its regard in spheres that include human rights, as is evidenced

FOR REFLECTION

The end of the Cold War (an accomplishment to which John Paul II contributed) probably means that the macro-economic debate between capitalism and communism is off the curriculum in most college courses.

So for current readers of this encyclical, this section about economic systems can reinforce John Paul II's ideas about private property, the common good, and mediating institutions like unions and families. In John Paul II's philosophy, the family (not the individual or the state) is the basic unit of society.

Catholic philosophy, John Paul II says in another encyclical, is not an ideological Third Way between capitalism and communism. It is, however, an alternative way of understanding society and social problems.

One political party in the United States promotes economic individualism, using slogans like "ownership society" and other ideological concepts. Another political party promotes cultural or lifestyle individualism, using a "right to choose" ideology.

- Is there a way to insert the insights of Catholic thinking into the delivery of social services in your area, into your consumer habits and your charitable giving, and maybe even into the platforms of political parties? Discuss how you might help this happen.

by the international declarations on work and the many labor codes prepared either by the competent legislative institutions in the various countries or by organizations devoting their social, or scientific and social, activity to the problems of work. One organization fostering such initiatives on the international level is the International Labor Organization, the oldest specialized agency of the United Nations.

In the following part of these considerations I intend to return in greater detail to these important questions, recalling at least the basic elements of the church's teaching on the matter. I must however first touch on a very important field of questions in which her teaching has taken shape in this latest period, the one marked and in a sense symbolized by the publication of the encyclical *Rerum Novarum.*

Throughout this period, which is by no means yet over, the issue of work has of course been posed on the basis of the great conflict that in the age of and together with industrial development emerged between "capital" and "labor," that is to say between the small but highly influential group of entrepreneurs, owners, or holders of the means of production, and the broader multitude of people who lacked these means and who shared in the process of production solely by their labor. The conflict originated in the fact that the workers put their powers at the disposal of the entrepreneurs and these, following the principle of maximum profit, tried to establish the lowest possible wages for the work done by the employees. In addition there were other elements of exploitation connected with the lack of safety at work and of safeguards regarding the health and living conditions of the workers and their families.

This conflict, interpreted by some as a socioeconomic class conflict, found expression in the ideological conflict between liberalism, understood as the ideology of capitalism, and Marxism, understood as the ideology of scientific socialism and communism, which professes to act as the spokesman for the working class and the worldwide proletariat. Thus the real conflict between labor and capital was transformed into a systematic class struggle conducted not only by ideological means, but also and chiefly by political means. We are familiar with the history of this conflict and with the demands of both sides. The Marxist program, based on the philosophy of Marx and Engels, sees in class struggle the only way to eliminate class injustices in society and to eliminate the classes themselves. Putting this program into practice presupposes the collectivization of the means of production so that, through the transfer of these means from private hands to the collectivity, human labor will be preserved from exploitation.

This is the goal of the struggle carried on by political as well as ideological means. In accordance with the principle of "the dictatorship of the proletariat," the groups that as political parties follow the guidance of Marxist ideology aim by the use of various kinds of influence, including revolutionary pressure, to win a monopoly of power in each society, in order to introduce the collectivist system into it by eliminating private ownership of the means of production. According to the principal ideologists and leaders of this broad international movement, the purpose of this program of action is to achieve social revolution and to introduce socialism and finally the communist system throughout the world.

As we touch on this extremely important field of issues, which constitute not only a theory but a whole fabric of socioeconomic, political, and international life in our age, we cannot go into the details, nor is this necessary, for they are known both from the vast literature on the subject and by experience. Instead we must leave the context of these issues and go back to the fundamental issue of human work, which is the main subject of the considerations in this document. It is clear indeed that this issue, which is of such importance for people—it constitutes one of the fundamental dimensions of earthly existence and of vocation—can also be explained only by taking into account the full context of the contemporary situation.

The Priority of Labor

The structure of the present-day situation is deeply marked by many conflicts caused by humankind, and the technological means produced by human work play a primary role in it. We should also consider here the prospect of worldwide catastrophe in the case of a nuclear war, which would have almost unimaginable possibilities of destruction. In view of this situation, we must first of all recall a principle that has always been taught by the church: the principle of the priority of labor over capital. This principle directly concerns the process of production: In this process labor is always a primary efficient cause, while capital, the whole collection of means of production, remains a mere instrument or instrumental cause. This principle is an evident truth that emerges from the whole of historical experience.

When we read in the first chapter of the Bible that people are to subdue the earth, we know that these works refer to all the resources contained in the visible world and placed at our disposal. However, these resources can serve humankind only through work. From the beginning there is also linked with work the question of ownership, for the only means that people have for causing the resources hidden in nature to serve them and others is work. And to be able through work to make these resources bear fruit, people take over ownership of small parts of the various riches of nature: those beneath the ground, those in the sea, on land, or in space. People take over all these things by making them a workbench. People take them over through work and for work.

The same principle applies in the successive phases of this process, in which the first phase always remains the relationship of people with the resources and riches of nature. The whole of the effort to acquire knowledge with the aim of discovering these riches and specifying the various ways in which they can be used by people and for people teaches us that everything that comes from people throughout the whole process of economic production, whether labor or the whole collection of means of production and the technology connected with these means (meaning the capability to use them in work), presupposes these riches and resources of the visible world, riches and resources that people find and do not create. In a sense people find them already prepared, ready for discovery and for correct use in the productive process. In every phase of the development of work people come up against the leading role of the gift made by "nature," that is to say, in the final analysis, by the Creator. At the beginning of work is the mystery of creation. This affirmation, already indicated as my starting point, is the guiding thread of this document and will be further developed in the last part of these reflections.

Further consideration of this question should confirm our conviction of the priority of human labor over what in the course of time we have grown accustomed to call capital. Since the concept of capital includes not only the natural resources placed at our disposal, but also the whole collection of means by which people appropriate natural resources and transform them in accordance with needs (and thus in a sense humanize them), it must immediately be noted that all these means are the result of the historical heritage of human labor. All the means of production, from the most primitive to the ultramodern one—it is people that have gradually developed them: human experience and intellect. In this way there have appeared not only the simplest instruments for cultivating the earth, but also through adequate progress in science and technology the more modern and complex

FOR REFLECTION

John Paul II addresses some economic issues in this encyclical. But his central concern is cultural: is there a way to conduct business, to exchange goods and services, to promote trade, to advance knowledge and discoveries so that labor is at the top of the agenda?

- Can you name any examples of a genuine work culture in the United States? If you can name them, discuss what makes them work. If you can't, why do you think that is?

- Is there any worthwhile art about work in contemporary culture?

- What art in your church or school celebrates the Christian dignity of work?

ones: machines, factories, laboratories, and computers. Thus everything that is at the service of work, everything that in the present state of technology constitutes its ever more highly perfected "instrument," is the result of work.

This gigantic and powerful instrument—the whole collection of means of production that in a sense are considered synonymous with "capital"—is the result of work and bears the signs of human labor. At the present stage of technological advance, when people, who are the subject of work, wish to make use of this collection of modern instruments, the means of production, they must first assimilate cognitively the result of the work of the people who invented those instruments, who planned them, built them, and perfected them, and who continue to do so. Capacity for work—that is to say, for sharing efficiently in the modern production process—demands greater and greater preparation and, before all else, proper training. Obviously it remains clear that every human being sharing in the production process, even if he or she is only doing the kind of work for which no special training or qualifications are required, is the real efficient subject in this production process, while the whole collection of instruments, no matter how perfect they may be in themselves, are only mere instruments subordinate to human labor.

This truth, which is part of the abiding heritage of the church's teaching, must always be emphasized with reference to the question of the labor system and with regard to the whole socioeconomic system. We must emphasize and give prominence to the primacy of the person in the production process, the primacy of people over things. Everything contained in the concept of capital in the strict sense is only a collection of things. The human being, as the subject of work and independent of the work done—the human being alone is a person. This principle is an evident truth that emerges from the whole of historical experience.

Economism and Materialism

In the light of the above truth we see clearly, first of all, that capital cannot be separated from labor; in no way can labor be opposed to capital or capital to labor, and still less can the actual people behind these concepts be opposed to each other, as will be explained later. A labor system can be right, in the sense of being in conformity with the very essence of the issue and in the sense of being intrinsically true and also morally legitimate, if in its very basis it overcomes the opposition between labor and capital through an effort at being shaped in accordance with the principle put forward above, the principle of the substantial and real priority of labor, of the subjectivity of human labor and its effective participation in the whole production process, independent of the nature of the services provided by the worker.

Opposition between labor and capital does not spring from the structure of the production process or from the structure of the economic process. In general the latter process demonstrates that labor and what we are accustomed to call capital are intermingled; it shows that they are inseparably linked. Working at any workbench, whether a relatively primitive or an ultramodern one, a person can easily see that through work he or she enters into two inheritances: the inheritance of what is given to the whole of humanity in the resources of nature and the inheritance of what others have already developed on the basis of those resources, primarily by developing technology, that is to say, by producing a whole collection of increasingly perfect instruments for work. In working, people also "enter into the labor of others."[21] Guided both by our intelligence and by the faith that draws light from the word of God, we have no difficulty in accepting this image, of the sphere and process of labor. It is a consistent image, one that is humanistic as well as theological. In it people are masters of the creatures placed at their disposal in the visible world. If some dependence is discovered in the work process, it is dependence on the Giver of all the resources of creation and also on other human beings, those to whose work and initiative we owe the perfected and increased possibilities of our own work. All that we can say of everything in the production process which constitutes a whole collection of "things," the instruments, the capital, is that it conditions work; we cannot assert that it constitutes as it were an impersonal "subject," putting people and work into a position of dependence.

This consistent image, in which the principle of the primacy of person over things is strictly preserved, was broken up in human thought sometime after a long period of incubation in practical living. The break occurred in such a way that labor was separated from capital and set in opposition to it, and capital was set in opposition to labor, as though they were two impersonal forces, two production factors juxtaposed in the same "economistic" perspective. This way of stating the issue contained a fundamental error; what we can call the error of economism, that of considering human labor solely according to its economic purpose. This fundamental error of thought can and must be called an error of materialism, in that economism directly or indirectly includes a conviction of the primacy and superiority of the material and, directly or indirectly, places the spiritual and the personal (human activity, moral values, and such matters) in a position of subordination to material reality. This is still not theoretical materialism in the full sense of the term, but it is certainly practical materialism, a materialism judged capable of satisfying human needs not so much on the grounds of premises derived from materialist theory as on the grounds of a particular way of evaluating things and so on the grounds of a certain hierarchy of goods based on the greater immediate attractiveness of what is material.

The error of thinking in the categories of economism went hand in hand with the formation of a materialist philosophy, as this philosophy developed from the most elementary and common phase (also called common materialism, because it professes to reduce spiritual reality to a superfluous phenomenon) to the phase of what is called dialectical materialism. However, within the framework of the present consideration, it seems that economism had a decisive importance for the fundamental issue of human work, in particular for the separation of labor and capital and for setting them up in opposition as two production factors viewed in the above-mentioned economistic perspective; and it seems that economism influenced this non-humanistic way of stating the issue before the materialist philosophical system did. Nevertheless it is obvious that materialism, including its dialectical form, is incapable of providing sufficient and definitive bases for thinking about human work, in order that the primacy of people over the capital instrument, the primacy of the person over things, may find in it adequate and irrefutable confirmation and support. In dialectical materialism too a person is not first and foremost the subject of work and the efficient cause of the production process, but continues to be understood and treated, in dependence on what is material, as a kind of "resultant" of the economic or production relations prevailing at a given period.

Obviously the antinomy between labor and capital under consideration here—the antinomy in which labor was separated from capital and set up in opposition to it, in a certain sense on the ontic level, as if it were just an element like any other in the economic process—did not originate merely in the philosophy and economic theories of the eighteenth century; rather it originated in the whole of economic and social practice of that time, the time of the birth and rapid development of industrialization, in which what was mainly seen was the possibility of vastly increasing material wealth, means, while the end, that is to say the human person, who should be served by the means, was ignored. It was this practical error that struck a blow first and foremost against human labor, against working people, and caused the ethically just social reaction already spoken of above. The same error, which is now part of history and which was connected with the period of primitive capitalism and liberalism, can nevertheless be repeated in other circumstances of time and place if people's thinking starts from the same theoretical or practical premises. The only chance there seems to be for radically overcoming this error is through adequate changes both in theory and in practice, changes in line with the definite conviction of the primacy of the person over things and of human labor over capital as a whole collection of means of production.

FOR REFLECTION

Many successful businesses, including those in the nonprofit sector, understand that dedicated and participatory employees greatly enhance productivity and delivery of services. The best companies consciously create an inclusive corporate culture, one in which employees have genuine responsibility.

At the same time, today's economy makes lifetime loyalty between a worker and a company unrealistic. A typical worker can expect to have three or more distinct careers and several jobs.

- How does your company include workers in the decision-making process?

- What is your experience with employee-of-the-month contests and other morale boosters at work?

Work and Ownership

The historical process briefly presented here has certainly gone beyond its initial phase, but it is still taking place and indeed is spreading in the relationships between nations and continents. It needs to be specified further from another point of view. It is obvious that when we speak of opposition between labor and capital, we are not dealing only with abstract concepts or "impersonal forces" operating in economic production. Behind both concepts there are people, living, actual people: On the one side are those who do the work without being the owners of the means of production, and on the other side those who act as entrepreneurs and who own these means or represent the owner. Thus the issue of ownership or property enters from the beginning into the whole of this difficult historical process. The encyclical *Rerum Novarum*, which has the social question as its theme, stresses this issue also, recalling and confirming the church's teaching on ownership, on the right to private property even when it is a question of the means of production. The encyclical *Mater et Magistra* did the same.

The above principle, as it was then stated and as it is still taught by the church, diverges radically from the program of collectivism as proclaimed by Marxism and put into practice in various countries in the decades following the time of Pope Leo XIII's encyclical. At the same time it differs from the program of capitalism practiced by liberalism and by the political systems inspired by it. In the latter case, the difference consists in the way the right to ownership or property is understood. Christian tradition has never upheld this right as absolute and untouchable. On the contrary, it has always understood this right within the broader context of the right common to all to use the goods of the whole of creation: The right to private property is subordinated to the right to common use, to the fact that goods are meant for everyone.

Furthermore, in the church's teaching, ownership has never been understood in a way that could constitute grounds for social conflict in labor. As mentioned above, property is acquired first of all through work in order that it may serve work. This concerns in a special way ownership of the means of production. Isolating these means as a separate property in order to set it up in the form of "capital" in opposition to "labor"—and even to practice exploitation of labor—is contrary to the very nature of these means and their possession. They cannot be possessed against labor, they cannot even be possessed for possession's sake, because the only legitimate title to their possession—whether in the form of private ownership or in the form of public or collective ownership—is that they should serve labor and thus by serving labor that they should make possible the achievement of the first principle of this order, namely the universal destination of goods and the right to common use of them. From this point of view, therefore, in consideration of human labor and of common access to goods, one cannot exclude the socialization, in suitable conditions, of certain means of production. In the course of the decades since the publication of the encyclical *Rerum Novarum*, the church's teaching has always recalled all these principles, going back to the arguments formulated in a much older tradition, for example, the well-known arguments of the *Summa Theologica* of St. Thomas Aquinas.[22]

In the present document, which has human work as its main theme, it is right to confirm all the effort with which the church's teaching has striven and continues to strive always to ensure the priority of work and thereby human character as a subject in social life and especially in the dynamic structure of the whole economic process. From this point of view the position of "rigid" capitalism continues to remain unacceptable, namely the position that defends the exclusive right to private ownership of the means of production as an untouchable "dogma" of economic life. The principle of respect for work demands that this right should undergo a constructive revision both in theory and in practice. If it is true that capital, as the whole of the means of production, is at the same time the product of the work of generations, it is equally true that capital is being unceasingly created through the work done with the help of all these means of production, and these means can be seen as a great workbench at which the present generation of workers is working day after day. Obviously we are dealing here with different kinds of work, not only so-called manual labor, but also the many forms of intellectual work, including white-collar work and management.

In the light of the above, the many proposals put forward by experts in Catholic social teaching and by the highest magisterium of the church take on special significance:[23] proposals for joint ownership of the means of work, sharing by the workers in the management and/ or profits of businesses, so-called shareholding by labor, and more.

Whether these various proposals can or cannot be applied concretely, it is clear that recognition of the proper position of labor and the worker in the production process demands various adaptations in the sphere of the right to ownership of the means of production. This is so not only in view of older situations but also, first and foremost, in view of the whole of the situation and the problems in the second half of the present century with regard to the so-called Third World and the various new independent countries that have arisen, especially in Africa but elsewhere as well, in place of the colonial territories of the past.

Therefore, while the position of "rigid" capitalism must undergo continual revision in order to be reformed from the point of view of human rights, both human rights in the widest sense and those linked with work, it must be stated that from the same point of view these many deeply desired reforms cannot be achieved by an *a priori* elimination of private ownership of the means of production. For it must be noted that merely taking these means of production (capital) out of the hands of their private owners is not enough to ensure their satisfactory socialization. They cease to be the property of a certain social group, namely the private owners, and become the property of organized society, coming under the administration and direct control of another group of people, namely those who, though not owning them, from the fact of exercising power in society manage them on the level of the whole national or the local economy.

This group in authority may carry out its task satisfactorily from the point of view of the priority of labor; but it may also carry it out badly by claiming for itself a monopoly of the administration and disposal of the means of production and not refraining even from offending basic human rights. Thus, merely converting the means of production into state property in the collectivist systems is by no means equivalent to "socializing" that property. We can speak of socializing only when the subject character of society is ensured, that is to say, when on the basis of work each person is fully entitled to consider himself or herself a part owner of the great workbench at which he or she is working with everyone else. A way toward that goal could be found by associating labor with the ownership of capital, as far as possible, and by producing a wide range of intermediate bodies with economic, social, and cultural purposes; they would be bodies enjoying real autonomy with regard to the public powers, pursuing their specific aims in honest collaboration with each other and in subordination to the demands of the common good, and they would be living communities both in form and in substance in the sense that the members of each body would be looked upon and treated as persons and encouraged to take an active part in the life of the body.[24]

The "Personalist" Argument

Thus, the principle of the priority of labor over capital is a postulate of the order of social morality. It has key importance both in the system built on the principle of private ownership of the means of production and also in the systems in which private ownership of these means has been limited even in a radical way. Labor is in a sense inseparable from capital; in no way does it accept the antinomy, that is to say, the separation and opposition with regard to the means of production that has weighed upon human life in recent centuries as a result of merely economic premises. When people work, using all the means of production, they also wish to use the fruit of this work and share it with others, and they wish to be able to take part in the very work process as a sharer in responsibility and creativity at the workbench to which they apply themselves.

From this spring certain specific rights of workers, corresponding to the obligation of work. They will be discussed later. But here it must be emphasized in general terms that the person who works desires not only due remuneration for work; that person also wishes that within the production process provision be made to be able to know that in work, even on something that is owned in common, that person is working "for himself or herself." This awareness is extinguished in a system of excessive bureaucratic centralization, which makes the worker feel like just a cog in a huge machine moved from above, that the worker is for more reasons than one a mere production instrument rather than a true subject of work with an initiative of his or her own. The church's teaching has always expressed the strong and deep conviction that work concerns not only the economy but also, and especially, personal values. The economic system itself and the production process benefit precisely when these personal values are fully respected. In the mind of St. Thomas Aquinas,[25] this is the principal reason in favor of private ownership of the means of production. While we accept that for certain well-founded reasons exceptions can be made to the principle of private ownership—in our own time we even see that the system of "socialized ownership" has been introduced—nevertheless the personalist argument still holds good both on the level of principles and on the practical level. If it is to be rational and fruitful, any socialization of the means of production must take this argument into consideration. Every effort must be made to ensure that in this kind of system also the human person can preserve awareness of working "for himself or herself." If this is not done, incalculable damage is inevitably done throughout the economic process, not only economic damage but first and foremost damage to the person.

IV. RIGHTS OF WORKERS

Within the Broad Context of Human Rights

While work, in all its many senses, is an obligation, that is to say a duty, it is also a source of rights on the part of the worker. These rights must be examined in the broad context of human rights as a whole, which are connatural and many of which are proclaimed by various international organizations and increasingly guaranteed by the individual states for their citizens. Respect for this broad range of human rights constitutes the fundamental condition for peace in the modern world: peace both within individual countries and societies and in international relations, as the church's magisterium has several times noted, especially since the encyclical *Pacem in Terris*. The human rights that flow from work are part of the broader context of those fundamental rights of the person.

However, within this context they have a specific character corresponding to the specific nature of human work as outlined above. It is in keeping with this character that we must view them. Work is, as has been said, an obligation, that is to say, a duty, on the part of people. This is true in all the many meanings of the word. People must work both because the Creator has commanded it and because of humanity, which requires work in order to be maintained and developed. People must work out of regard for others, especially their own family, but also for the society, to the country of which they are children and the whole human family of which they are members, since each person is the heir to the work of generations and at the same time a sharer in building the future of those who will come after in the succession of history. All this constitutes the moral obligation of work understood in its wide sense. When we have to consider the moral rights corresponding to this obligation of every person with regard to work, we must always keep before our eyes the whole vast range of points of reference in which the labor of every working subject is manifested.

For when we speak of the obligation of work and of the rights of the worker that correspond to this obligation, we think in the first place of the relationship between the employer, direct or indirect, and the worker.

The distinction between the direct and the indirect employer is seen to be very important when one considers both the way in which labor is actually organized and the possibility of the formation of just or unjust relationships in the field of labor.

Since the direct employer is the person or institution with whom the worker enters directly into a work contract in accordance with definite

conditions, we must understand as the indirect employer many different factors, other than the direct employer, that exercise a determining
influence on the shaping both of the work contract and consequently
of just or unjust relationships in the field of human labor.

Direct and Indirect Employer

The concept of indirect employer includes both persons and institutions of various kinds and also collective labor contracts and the
principles of conduct which are laid down by these persons and institutions and which determine the whole socioeconomic system or
are its result. The concept of "indirect employer" thus refers to many
different elements. The responsibility of the indirect employer differs from that of the direct employer—the term itself indicates that
the responsibility is less direct—but it remains a true responsibility:
The indirect employer substantially determines one or other facet of
the labor relationship, thus conditioning the conduct of the direct
employer when the latter determines in concrete terms the actual
work contract and labor relations. This is not to absolve the direct
employer from responsibility, but only to draw attention to the whole
network of influences that condition conduct. When it is a question
of establishing an ethically correct labor policy, all these influences
must be kept in mind. A policy is correct when the objective rights of
the worker are fully respected.

The concept of indirect employer is applicable to every society and
in the first place to the state. For it is the state that must conduct a
just labor policy. However, it is common knowledge that in the present
system of economic relations in the world there are numerous links
between individual states, links that find expression, for instance, in
the import and export process, that is to say, in the mutual exchange
of economic goods, whether raw materials, semi-manufactured goods,
or finished industrial products. These links also create mutual dependence, and as a result it would be difficult to speak in the case of any

state, even the economically most powerful, of complete self-sufficiency or autarky.

Such a system of mutual dependence is in itself normal. However it can easily become an occasion for various forms of exploitation or injustice and as a result influence the labor policy of individual states; and finally it can influence the individual worker who is the proper subject of labor. For instance the highly industrialized countries, and even more the businesses that direct on a large scale the means of industrial production (the companies referred to as multinational or transnational), fix the highest possible prices for their products, while trying at the same time to fix the lowest possible prices for raw materials or semi-manufactured goods. This is one of the causes of an ever-increasing disproportion between national incomes. The gap between most of the richest countries and the poorest ones is not diminishing or being stabilized, but is increasing more and more to the detriment, obviously, of the poor countries. Evidently this must have an effect on local labor policy and on the worker's situation in the economically disadvantaged societies. Being in a system thus conditioned, the direct employer fixes working conditions below the objective requirements of the workers, especially if the employer wishes to obtain the highest possible profits from the business (or from the businesses which he or she runs, in the case of a situation of "socialized" ownership of the means of production).

It is easy to see that this framework of forms of dependence linked with the concept of the indirect employer is enormously extensive and complicated. It is determined, in a sense, by all the elements that are decisive for economic life within a given society and state, but also by much wider links and forms of dependence. The attainment of the worker's rights cannot however be [deemed] to be merely a result of economic systems, which on a larger or smaller scale are guided chiefly by the criterion of maximum profit. On the contrary, it is respect for the objective rights of the worker—every kind of worker: manual or intellectual, industrial or agricultural, and others—that must constitute the adequate and fundamental criterion for shaping the whole economy, both on the level of the individual society and state and within the whole of the world economic policy and of the systems of international relationships that derive from it.

Influence in this direction should be exercised by all the international organizations whose concern it is, beginning with the United Nations. It appears that the International Labor Organization and the Food and Agriculture Organization of the United Nations and other bodies too have fresh contributions to offer on this point in particular. Within the individual states there are ministries or public departments and also various social institutions set up for this purpose. All of this effectively indicates the importance of the indirect employer—as has been said above—in achieving full respect for the worker's rights, since the rights of the human person are the key element in the whole of the social moral order.

The Employment Issue

When we consider the rights of workers in relation to the "indirect employer," that is to say, all the agents at the national and international level that are responsible for the whole orientation of labor policy, we must first direct our attention to a fundamental issue: the question of finding work or, in other words, the issue of suitable employment for all who are capable of it. The opposite of a just and right situation in this field is unemployment, that is to say, the lack of work for those who are capable of it. It can be a question of general unemployment or of unemployment in certain sectors of work. The role of the agents included under the title of indirect employer is to act against unemployment, which in all cases is an evil, and which when it reaches a certain level can become a real social disaster. It is particularly painful when it especially affects young people, who after appropriate cultural, technical, and professional preparation fail to find work and see their sincere wish to work and their readiness to take on their own responsibility for the economic and social development of the community sadly frustrated. The obligation to provide unemployment benefits, that is to say, the duty to make suitable grants indispensable for the subsistence of unemployed workers and their families, is a duty springing from the fundamental principle of the moral order in this sphere, namely the principle of the common use of goods or, to put it in another and still simpler way, the right to life and subsistence.

In order to meet the danger of unemployment and to ensure employment for all, the agents defined here as "indirect employer" must make provision for overall planning with regard to the different kinds of work by which not only the economic life, but also the cultural life of a given society is shaped; they must also give attention to organizing that work in a correct and rational way. In the final analysis this overall concern weighs on the shoulders of the state, but it cannot mean one-sided centralization by the public authorities. Instead, what is in question is a just and rational coordination, within the framework of which the initiative of individuals, free groups, and local work centers and complexes must be safeguarded, keeping in mind what has been said above with regard to the subject character of human labor.

The fact of the mutual dependence of societies and states and the need to collaborate in various areas mean that, while preserving the sovereign rights of each society and state in the field of planning and organizing labor in its own society, action in this important area must also be taken in the dimension of international collaboration by means of the necessary treaties and agreements. Here too the criterion for these pacts and agreements must more and more be the criterion of human work considered as a fundamental right of all human beings, work which gives similar rights to all those who work in such a way that the living standard of the workers in the different societies will less and less show those disturbing differences which are unjust and are apt to provoke even violent reactions. The international organizations have an enormous part to play in this area. They must let themselves be guided by an exact diagnosis of the complex situations and of the

FOR REFLECTION

The Didache, among the earliest Christian writings, challenges the Christian community to create employment, especially for new converts. St. Thomas Aquinas, writing many years later, says that expanding the possibilities for worthwhile jobs is the virtue of magnanimity in practice.

- An individual Christian routinely passes along job leads to unemployed friends. An individual Christian frequently donates clothes or food to agencies that assist the unemployed. A few parishes even have a support and job referral ministry for the unemployed. But what about when you are not a volunteer, when you are "on the clock": How can you help your company expand in such a way that it hires more workers?

- Can you, through your union, professional association, or political party, help your city grow richer through increased employment? In what specific ways?

influence exercised by natural, historical, civil, and other such circumstances. They must also be more highly operative with regard to plans for action jointly decided on, that is to say, they must be more effective in carrying them out.

In this direction, it is possible to actuate a plan for universal and proportionate progress by all in accordance with the guidelines of Pope Paul VI's encyclical *Populorum Progressio*. It must be stressed that the constitutive element in this progress and also the most adequate way to verify it in a spirit of justice and peace, which the church proclaims and for which she does not cease to pray to the Father of all individuals and of all peoples, is the continual reappraisal of work, both in the aspect of its objective finality and in the aspect of the dignity of the subject of all work, that is to say, the human person. The progress in question must be made through workers and for workers and it must produce its fruit in people. A test of this progress will be the increasingly mature recognition of the purpose of work and increasingly universal respect for the rights inherent in work in conformity with the dignity of each person, the subject of work.

Rational planning and the proper organization of human labor in keeping with individual societies and states should also facilitate the discovery of the right proportions between the different kinds of employment: work on the land, in industry, in the various services, white-collar work and scientific or artistic work, in accordance with the capacities of individuals and for the common good of each society and of the whole of humankind. The organization of human life in accordance with the many possibilities of labor should be matched by a suitable system of instruction and education aimed first of all at

FOR REFLECTION

A particular workplace might be quite harmonious. The owners or managers go beyond the norm in their consideration for the employees, including situations at home. While progressive management is laudable and often results in fine productivity, it is not the best lens for verifying the justice of a company. The proper relationship between an employer and the workers is, says John Paul II, best clarified with a just wage.

- Sometimes an employer, particularly a nonprofit agency (including the Roman Catholic Church), pays below-market wages because its mission is humanitarian. Sometimes a worker agrees to a below-market wage because the job fulfills his or her vocation. Are the intentions of an employer or a worker relevant in determining exploitation? Why or why not?

developing mature human beings, but also aimed at preparing people specifically for assuming to good advantage an appropriate place in the vast and socially differentiated world of work.

As we view the whole human family throughout the world, we cannot fail to be struck by a disconcerting fact of immense proportions: the fact that while conspicuous natural resources remain unused, there are huge numbers of people who are unemployed or underemployed and countless multitudes of people suffering from hunger. This is a fact that without any doubt demonstrates that both within the individual political communities and in their relationships on the continental and world level there is something wrong with the organization of work and employment, precisely at the most critical and socially most important points.

Wages and Other Social Benefits

After outlining the important role that concern for providing employment for all workers plays in safeguarding respect for inalienable rights in view of work, it is worthwhile taking a closer look at these rights, which in the final analysis are formed within the relationship between worker and direct employer. All that has been said above on the subject of the indirect employer is aimed at defining these relationships more exactly, by showing the many forms of conditioning within which these relationships are indirectly formed. This consideration does not however have a purely descriptive purpose; it is not a brief treatise on economics or politics. It is a matter of highlighting the deontological and moral aspect. The key problem of social ethics in this case is that of just remuneration for work done. In the context of the present, there is no more important way for securing a just relationship between the worker and the employer than that constituted by remuneration for work. Whether the work is done in a system of private ownership of the means of production or in a system where ownership has undergone a certain "socialization," the relationship between the employer (first and foremost the direct employer) and the worker is resolved on the basis of the wage, that is, through just remuneration of the work done.

It should also be noted that the justice of a socioeconomic system and, in each case, its just functioning, deserve in the final analysis to be evaluated by the way in which work is properly remunerated in the system. Here we return once more to the first principle of the whole ethical and social order, namely the principle of the common use of goods. In every system, regardless of the fundamental relationships within it between capital and labor, wages, that is to say remuneration for work, are still a practical means whereby the vast majority of people can have access to those goods which are intended for common use: both the goods of nature and manufactured goods. Both kinds of goods become accessible to the worker through the wage received as remuneration for work. Hence in every case a just wage is the concrete means of verifying the justice of the whole socioeconomic system and, in any case, of checking that it is functioning justly. It is not the only means of checking, but it is a particularly important one and in a sense the key means.

This means of checking concerns above all the family. Just remuneration for the work of an adult who is responsible for a family means remuneration that will suffice for establishing and properly maintaining a family and for providing security for its future. Such remuneration can be given either through what is called a family wage—that is, a single salary given to the head of the family, sufficient for the needs of the family without the other spouse having to take up gainful employment outside the home—or through other social measures such as family allowances or grants to mothers devoting themselves exclusively to their families. These grants should correspond to the actual needs, that is, to the number of dependents for as long as they are not in a position to assume proper responsibility for their own lives.

Experience confirms that there must be a social re-evaluation of the mother's role, of the toil connected with it, and of the need that children have for care, love, and affection in order that they may develop into responsible, morally and religiously mature, and psychologically stable persons. It will redound to the credit of society to make it possible for a mother—without inhibiting her freedom, without psychological or practical discrimination, and without penalizing her as compared with other women—to devote herself to taking care of her children and educating them in accordance with their needs, which vary with age. Having to abandon these tasks in order to take up paid work outside the home is wrong from the point of view of the good of society and of the family when it contradicts or hinders these primary goals of the mission of a mother.[26]

In this context it should be emphasized that on a more general level the whole labor process must be organized and adapted in such a way as to respect the requirements of the person and his or her forms of life, above all life in the home, taking into account the individual's age and sex. It is a fact that in many societies women work in nearly every sector of life. But it is fitting that they should be able to fulfill their tasks in accordance with their own nature, without being discriminated against and without being excluded from jobs for which they are capable, but also without lack of respect for their family aspirations and for their specific role in contributing, together with men, to the good of society. The true advancement of women requires that labor should be structured in such a way that women do not have to pay for their advancement by abandoning what is specific to them and at the expense of the family, in which women as mothers have an irreplaceable role.

Besides wages, various social benefits intended to ensure the life and health of workers and their families play a part here. The expenses involved in health care, especially in the case of accidents at work, demand that medical assistance should be easily available for workers and that as far as possible it should be cheap or even free of charge. Another sector regarding benefits is the sector associated with the right to rest. In the first place this involves a regular weekly rest comprising at least Sunday and also a longer period of rest, namely the holiday or vacation taken once a year or possibly in several shorter periods during the year. A third sector concerns the right to a pension and to insurance for old age and in case of accidents at work. Within the sphere of these principal rights there develops a whole system of particular rights which, together with remuneration for work, determine the correct relationship between worker and employer. Among these rights there should never be overlooked the right to a working environment and to manufacturing processes which are not harmful to the workers' physical health or to their moral integrity.

FOR REFLECTION

Labor unions, says John Paul II, are indispensable for structuring a just society and fostering human solidarity.

Each union, of course, advocates for its members. Additionally, a multiplicity of unions, along with other mediating structures, make it less likely that individuals will have to negotiate the harsh edges of economic and political life on their own. Unions, as one example of the Catholic doctrine on subsidiarity, make it more likely that people will relate to one another on a personal basis and will be confident in exercising freedom in a responsible manner.

- How well is the Catholic doctrine on unions known in your parish or among your circle of Catholic friends, in your office or jobsite? How might you spread the word?

Importance of Unions

All these rights, together with the need for the workers themselves to secure them, give rise to yet another right: the right of association, that is, to form associations for the purpose of defending the vital interests of those employed in the various professions. These associations are called labor or trade unions. The vital interests of the workers are to a certain extent common for all of them; at the same time, however, each type of work, each profession, has its own specific character which should find a particular reflection in these organizations.

In a sense, unions go back to the medieval guilds of artisans, insofar as those organizations brought together people belonging to the same craft and thus on the basis of their work. However unions differ from the guilds on this essential point: The modern unions grew up from the struggle of the workers—workers in general but especially the industrial workers—to protect their just rights vis-à-vis the entrepreneurs and the owners of the means of production. Their task is to defend the existential interests of workers in all sectors in which their rights are concerned. The experience of history teaches that organizations of this type are an indispensable element of social life, especially in modern industrialized societies. Obviously this does not mean that only industrial workers can set up associations of this type. Representatives of every profession can use them to ensure their own rights. Thus there are unions of agricultural workers and of white-collar workers; there are also employers' associations. All, as has been said above, are further divided into groups or subgroups according to particular professional specializations.

Catholic social teaching does not hold that unions are no more than a reflection of the "class" structure of society and that they are a mouthpiece for a class struggle that inevitably governs social life. They are indeed a mouthpiece for the struggle for social justice, for the just rights of working people in accordance with their individual professions. However, this struggle should be seen as a normal endeavor "for" the just good: In the present case, for the good which corresponds to the needs and merits of working people associated by profession; but it is not a struggle "against" others. Even if in controversial questions the struggle takes on a character of opposition toward others, this is because it aims at the good of social justice, not for the sake of "struggle" or in order to eliminate the opponent. It is characteristic of work that it first and foremost unites people. In this consists its social power: the power to build a community. In the final analysis, both those who work and those who manage the means of production or who own them must in some way be united in this community. In the light of this fundamental structure of all work—in the light of the fact that, in the final analysis, labor and capital are indispensable components of the process of production in any social system—it is clear that even if it is because of their work needs that people unite to secure their rights, their union remains a constructive factor of social order and solidarity, and it is impossible to ignore it.

Just efforts to secure the rights of workers who are united by the same profession should always take into account the limitations imposed by the general economic situation of the country. Union demands cannot be turned into a kind of group or class "egoism," although they can and should also aim at correcting—with a view to the common good of the whole of society—everything defective in the system of ownership of the means of production or in the way these are managed. Social and socioeconomic life is certainly like a system of "connected vessels," and every social activity directed toward safeguarding the rights of particular groups should adapt itself to this system.

In this sense, union activity undoubtedly enters the field of politics, understood as prudent concern for the common good. However, the role of unions is not to "play politics" in the sense that the expression is commonly understood today. Unions do not have the character of political parties struggling for power; they should not be subjected to the decision of political parties or have too close links with them. In fact, in such a situation they easily lose contact with their specific role, which is to secure the just rights of workers within the framework of the common good of the whole of society; instead they become an instrument used for other purposes.

Speaking of the protection of the just rights of workers according to their individual professions, we must, of course, always keep in mind that which determines the subjective character of work in each profession, but at the same time, indeed before all else, we must keep in mind that which conditions the specific dignity of the subject of the work. The activity of union organizations opens up many possibilities in this respect, including their efforts to instruct and educate the workers and to foster education. Praise is due to the work of the schools, what are known as workers' or people's universities and the training programs and courses which have developed and are still developing this field of activity. It is always to be hoped that, thanks to the work of their unions, workers will not only *have* more, but above all *be* more: in other words, that they will realize their humanity more fully in every respect.

One method used by unions in pursuing the just rights of their members is the strike or work stoppage, as a kind of ultimatum to the competent bodies, especially the employers. This method is recognized by Catholic social teaching as legitimate in the proper conditions and within just limits. In this connection workers should be assured the right to strike, without being subjected to personal penal sanctions for taking part in a strike. While admitting that it is a legitimate means, we must at the same time emphasize that a strike remains, in a sense, an extreme means. It must not be abused; it must not be abused especially for "political" purposes. Furthermore, it must never be forgotten that when essential community services are in question, they must in every case be ensured, if necessary by means of appropriate legislation. Abuse of the strike weapon can lead to the paralysis of the whole of socioeconomic life, and this is contrary to the requirements of the common good of society, which also corresponds to the properly understood nature of work itself....

V. ELEMENTS FOR A SPIRITUALITY OF WORK

A Particular Task for the Church

It is right to devote the last part of these reflections about human work on the occasion of the ninetieth anniversary of the encyclical *Rerum Novarum* to the spirituality of work in the Christian sense. Since work in its subjective aspect is always a personal action, an *actus personae,* it follows that the whole person, body and spirit, participates in it, whether it is manual or intellectual work. It is also to the whole person that the word of the living God is directed, the evangelical message of salvation in which we find many points that concern human work and throw particular light on it. These points need to be properly assimilated: An inner effort on the part of the human spirit, guided by faith, hope, and charity, is needed in order that through these points the work of the individual human being may be given the meaning which it has in the eyes of God and by means of which work enters into the salvation process on a par with the other ordinary yet particularly important components of its texture.

The church considers it her duty to speak out on work from the viewpoint of its human value and of the moral order to which it belongs, and she sees this as one of her important tasks within the service that she renders to the evangelical message as a whole. At the same time she sees it as her particular duty to form a spirituality of work which will help all people to come closer, through work, to God, the Creator and Redeemer, to participate in salvation for humankind and the world, and to deepen their friendship with Christ in their lives by accepting, through faith, a living participation in his threefold mission as priest, prophet, and king, as the Second Vatican Council so eloquently teaches.

FOR REFLECTION

Whenever the word "spirituality" is used in the United States it invariably is associated with an individual's one-to-one relationship with God (or with a Higher Power or with "one's true self"). It is as if spirituality is one more consumer item.

Spirituality also usually means a deliberately prayerful break with the daily routine.

John Paul II's spirituality of work (no, it is not an oxymoron) is more like a way of life that integrates business, family life, and civic involvement with fidelity to Jesus' gospel. Spirituality, John Paul II seems to say, is not entirely something one does. It is to some degree something that is already embedded in the culture of your city, your workplace, and your home. This spirituality of work, as suggested by our milieu, is probably noisy, pluralistic, active, and very communal.

- What are your motives for going to work in the morning (or evening)? Is one motive usually stronger than the others?

- Is it necessary to additionally spiritualize work in some way? Is there, to ask the question differently, any such thing as a Christian auto dealership, a Christian insurance agency, or a Christian rock concert?

Work as a Sharing in the Activity of the Creator

As the Second Vatican Council says, "Throughout the course of the centuries, people have labored to better the circumstances of their lives through a monumental amount of individual and collective effort. To believers, this point is settled: Considered in itself, such human activity accords with God's will. For people, created to God's image, received a mandate to subject to them the earth and all that it contains, and to govern the world with justice and holiness; a mandate to relate humankind and the totality of things to him who was to be acknowledged as the Lord and Creator of all. Thus, by the subjection of all things to them, the name of God would be wonderful in all the earth."[27]

The word of God's revelation is profoundly marked by the fundamental truth that people, created in the image of God, share by work in the activity of the Creator and that, within the limits of human capabilities, people in a sense continue to develop that activity and perfect it as they advance further and further in the discovery of the resources and values contained in the whole of creation. We find this truth at the very beginning of sacred scripture in the Book of Genesis, where the creation activity itself is presented in the form of "work" done by God during "six days,"[28] "resting" on the seventh day.[29] Besides, the last book of sacred scripture echoes the same respect for what God has done through creative "work" when it proclaims: "Great and wonderful are your deeds, O Lord God the Almighty"[30]; this is similar to the Book of Genesis, which concludes the description of each day of creation with the statement: "And God saw that it was good."[31]

This description of creation, which we find in the very first chapter of the Book of Genesis, is also in a sense the first "gospel of work." For it shows what the dignity of work consists of: It teaches that people ought to imitate God, our Creator, in working, because people alone have the unique characteristic of likeness to God. People ought to imitate God both in working and also in resting, since God wished to present God's own creative activity under the form of work and rest. This activity by God in the world always continues, as the words of Christ attest: "My father is working still";[32] he works with creative power by sustaining in existence the world that he called into being from nothing, and he works with salvific power in the hearts of those whom from the beginning he has destined for "rest"[33] in union with himself in his "Father's house."[34] Therefore human work too not only requires a rest every "seventh day,"[35] but also cannot consist in the mere exercise of human strength in external action; it must leave room for workers to prepare themselves, by becoming more and more what in the will of God they ought to be, for the "rest" that the Lord reserves for his servants and friends.[36]

Awareness that human work is a participation in God's activity ought to permeate, as the Council teaches, even "the most ordinary everyday activities. For, while providing the substance of life for themselves and their families, men and women are performing their activities in a way that appropriately benefits society. They can justly consider that by their labor they are unfolding the Creator's work, consulting the advantages of their brothers and sisters, and contributing by their personal industry to the realization in history of the divine plan."[37]

This Christian spirituality of work should be a heritage shared by all. Especially in the modern age, the spirituality of work should show the maturity called for by the tensions and restlessness of mind and heart. "Far from thinking that works produced by human talent and energy are in opposition to God's power, and that the rational creature exists as a kind of rival to the Creator, Christians are convinced that the triumphs of the human race are a sign of God's greatness and the flowering of God's own mysterious design. For the greater human power becomes, the farther individual and community responsibility extends.... People are not deterred by the Christian message from building up the world or impelled to neglect the welfare of their fellows. They are, rather, more stringently bound to do these very things."[38]

The knowledge that by means of work people share in the work of creation constitutes the most profound motive for undertaking it in various sectors. "The faithful, therefore," we read in the constitution *Lumen Gentium*, "must learn the deepest meaning and the value of all creation, and its orientation to the praise of God. Even by their secular activity they must assist one another to live holier lives. In this way the world will be permeated by the spirit of Christ and more effectively achieve its purpose in justice, charity, and peace.... Therefore, by their competence in secular fields and by their personal activity, elevated from within by the grace of Christ, let them work vigorously so that by human labor, technical skill, and civil culture, created goods may be perfected according to the design of the Creator and the light of his word."[39]

FOR REFLECTION

Over forty different occupations are mentioned in the New Testament. Obviously, St. Paul and the evangelists derived metaphors and lessons from the workaday world in their proclamation of the Christian story.

■ How does the preaching in your parish relate the liturgy of the Word to the liturgy of the world, the world of work? How might you help your homilist relate his message to the world of work?

Christ, the Man of Work

The truth that by means of work people participate in the activity of God, our Creator, was given particular prominence by Jesus Christ—the Jesus at whom many of his first listeners in Nazareth "were astonished, saying, 'Where did this man get all this? What is the wisdom given to him?...Is not this the carpenter?'"[40] For Jesus not only proclaimed, but first and foremost fulfilled by his deeds the "gospel," the word of eternal wisdom that had been entrusted to him. Therefore, this was also "the gospel of work," because he who proclaimed it was himself a man of work, a craftsman like Joseph of Nazareth.[41] And if we do not find in his words a special command to work—but rather on one occasion a prohibition against too much anxiety about work and life[42]—at the same time the eloquence of the life of Christ is unequivocal: He belongs to the "working world," he has appreciation and respect for human work. It can indeed be said that he looks with love upon human work and the different forms that it takes, seeing in each one of these forms a particular facet of our likeness with God, the Creator and Father. Is it not he who says: "My Father is the vinedresser,"[43] and in various ways puts into his teaching the fundamental truth about work which is already expressed in the whole tradition of the Old Testament, beginning with the Book of Genesis?

The books of the Old Testament contain many references to human work and to the individual professions exercised by man: for example, the doctor,[44] the pharmacist,[45] the craftsman or artist,[46] the blacksmith[47]—we could apply these words to today's foundry workers—the potter,[48] the farmer,[49] the scholar,[50] the sailor,[51] the builder,[52] the musician,[53] the shepherd,[54] and the fisherman.[55] The words of praise for the work of women are well known.[56] In his parables on the kingdom of God, Jesus Christ constantly refers to human work: that of the shepherd,[57] the farmer,[58] the doctor,[59] the sower,[60] the householder,[61] the servant,[62] the steward,[63] the fisherman,[64] the merchant,[65] the laborer.[66] He also speaks of the various forms of women's work.[67] He compares the apostolate to the manual work of harvesters[68] or fishermen.[69] He refers to the work of scholars too.[70]

This teaching of Christ on work, based on the example of his life during his years in Nazareth, finds a particularly lively echo in the teaching of the apostle Paul. Paul boasts of working at his trade (he was probably a tentmaker),[71] and thanks to that work he was able even as an apostle to earn his own bread.[72] "With toil and labor we worked night and day, that we might not burden any of you."[73] Hence his instructions, in the form of exhortation and command, on the subject of work: "Now such persons we command and exhort in the Lord Jesus Christ to do their work in quietness and to earn their own living," he writes to the Thessalonians.[74] In fact, noting that some "are living in idleness…, not doing any work,"[75] the apostle does not hesitate to say in the same context: "If any one will not work, let them not eat."[76] In another passage he encourages his readers: "Whatever your task, work heartily, as serving the Lord and not for others, knowing that from the Lord you will receive the inheritance as your reward."[77]

The teachings of the "apostle of the gentiles" obviously have key importance for the morality and spirituality of human work. They are an important complement to the great though discreet gospel of work that we find in the life and parables of Christ, in what Jesus "did and taught."[78]

On the basis of these illuminations emanating from the source himself, the church has always proclaimed what we find expressed in modern terms in the teaching of the Second Vatican Council: "Just as human activity proceeds from people, so it is ordered toward people. For when a people work they not only alter things and society, they develop themselves as well. They learn much, they cultivate resources, they go outside of themselves and beyond themselves. Rightly understood, this kind of growth is of greater value than any external riches which can be garnered....Hence, the norm of human activity is this: that in accord with the divine plan and will, it should harmonize with the genuine good of the human race and allow people as individuals and as members of society to pursue their total vocation and fulfill it."[79]

Such a vision of the values of human work, or in other words such a spirituality of work, fully explains what we read in the same section of the Council's pastoral constitution with regard to the right meaning of progress: "A person is more precious for what he or she is than for what he or she has. Similarly, all that people do to obtain greater justice, wider brotherhood, and a more humane ordering of social relationships has greater worth than technical advances. For these advances can supply the material for human progress, but of themselves alone they can never actually bring it about."[80]

This teaching on the question of progress and development—a subject that dominates present-day thought—can be understood only as the fruit of a tested spirituality of human work; and it is only on the basis of such a spirituality that it can be realized and put into practice. This is the teaching and also the program that has its roots in "the gospel of work."

FOR REFLECTION

Work has too often become individualized careerism, says Michael Naughton of the University of St. Thomas. Similarly, leisure is restricted to individualized entertainment or amusement.

Just as John Paul II invites us to think of work as a vocation, he believes true leisure is a form of contemplation.

- On what day of the workweek do you start "waiting for the weekend"? What is it that you value in the "weekend"?

- Is your weekend more work than leisure? In what ways?

Human Work in the Light of the Cross and the Resurrection of Christ

There is yet another aspect of human work, an essential dimension of it, that is profoundly imbued with the spirituality based on the gospel. All work, whether manual or intellectual, is inevitably linked with toil. The Book of Genesis expresses it in a truly penetrating manner: The original blessing of work contained in the very mystery of creation and connected with our elevation as the image of God is contrasted with the curse that sin brought with it: "Cursed is the ground because of you; in toil you shall eat of it all the days of your life."[81] This toil connected with work marks the way of human life on earth and constitutes an announcement of death: "In the sweat of your face you shall eat bread till you return to the ground, for out of it you were taken."[82] Almost as an echo of these words, the author of one of the Wisdom books says: "Then I considered all that my hands had done and the toil I had spent in doing it."[83] There is no one on earth who could not apply these words to himself or herself.

In a sense, the final word of the gospel on this matter as on others is found in the paschal mystery of Jesus Christ. It is here that we must seek an answer to these problems so important for the spirituality of human work. The paschal mystery contains the cross of Christ and his obedience unto death, which the apostle contrasts with the disobedience which from the beginning has burdened our history on earth.[84] It also contains the elevation of Christ, who by means of death on a cross returns to his disciples in the resurrection with the power of the Holy Spirit.

Sweat and toil, which work necessarily involves in the present condition of the human race, present the Christian and everyone who is called to follow Christ with the possibility of sharing lovingly in the work that Christ came to do.[85] This work of salvation came about through suffering and death on a cross. By enduring the toil of work in union with Christ crucified for us, we in a way collaborate with the Son of God for the redemption of humanity. We show ourselves [to be] a true disciple of Christ by carrying the cross in turn every day[86] in the activity that we are called upon to perform.

Christ, "undergoing death itself for all of us sinners, taught us by example that we too must shoulder that cross which the world and the flesh inflict upon those who pursue peace and justice;" but also, at the same time, "appointed Lord by his resurrection and given all authority in heaven and on earth, Christ is now at work in people's hearts through the power of his Spirit.…He animates, purifies, and strengthens those noble longings too by which the human family strives to make its life more human and to render the whole earth submissive to this goal."[87]

The Christian finds in human work a small part of the cross of Christ and accepts it in the same spirit of redemption in which Christ accepted his cross for us. In work, thanks to the light that penetrates us from the resurrection of Christ, we always find a glimmer of new life, of the new good, as if it were an announcement of "the new heavens and the new earth"[88] in which we and the world participate precisely through the toil that goes with work. Through toil—and never without it. On the one hand this confirms the indispensability of the cross in the spirituality of human work; on the other hand the cross, which this toil constitutes, reveals a new good springing from work itself, from work understood in depth and in all its aspects and never apart from work.

Is this new good—the fruit of human work—already a small part of that "new earth" where justice dwells?[89] If it is true that the many forms of toil that go with work are a small part of the cross of Christ, what is the relationship of this new good to the resurrection of Christ?

The Council seeks to reply to this question also, drawing light from the very sources of the revealed word: "Therefore, while we are warned that it profits a man nothing if he gains the whole world and loses himself (cf. Luke 9:25), the expectation of a new earth must not weaken but rather stimulate our concern for cultivating this one. For here grows the body of a new human family, a body which even now is able to give some kind of foreshadowing of the new age. Earthly progress must be carefully distinguished from the growth of Christ's kingdom. Nevertheless, to the extent that the former can contribute to the better ordering of human society, it is of vital concern to the kingdom of God."[90]

In these present reflections devoted to human work we have tried to emphasize everything that seemed essential to it, since it is through labor that not only "the fruits of our activity," but also "human dignity, brotherhood, and freedom" must increase on earth.[91] Let the Christian who listens to the word of the living God, uniting work with prayer, know the place that work has not only in earthly progress, but also in the development of the kingdom of God, to which we are all called through the power of the Holy Spirit and through the word of the gospel.

In concluding these reflections, I gladly impart the apostolic blessing to all of you, venerable brothers and beloved sons and daughters.

I prepared this document for publication last May 15, on the ninetieth anniversary of the encyclical *Rerum Novarum*, but it is only after my stay in the hospital that I have been able to revise it definitively.

Given at Castelgandolfo, September 14, the Feast of the Triumph of the Cross, in the year 1981, the third of the pontificate.

FOR REFLECTION

John Paul II proclaimed the gospel of work in hundreds of sermons, in books, in articles, in poems, and more. His metaphors are compelling; his vision is inspiring; his issues are very timely. But his message—indeed the entire body of Catholic social philosophy—often remains a topic for specialists or a curiosity for historians.

The power of John Paul II's message will only come alive when we devise rituals that make the good news of work a vibrant part of our imaginations.

- What rituals can you use in your workplace to remind you of the sacredness of your work?

- What rituals could occur at your parish to help all its members, particularly its young adults, appreciate the importance of good work?

- How can your parish's "liturgy" (from a Greek word meaning the work of the people) be celebrated in a way that sends you out for your crucial work in the world, Monday through Saturday?

ENDNOTES

1. Cf. Psalm 127 (128):2; cf. also Genesis 3:17–19; Proverbs 10:22; Exodus 1:8–14; Jeremiah 22:13

2. Cf. Genesis 1:26

3. Cf. Genesis 1:28

4. Encyclical *Redemptor Hominis*, 14

5. Cf. Psalm 127 (128):2

6. Genesis 3:19

7. Cf. Matthew 13:52

8. Second Vatican Council, Pastoral Constitution on the Church in the Modern World, *Gaudium et Spes*, 38

9. Genesis 1:27

10. Genesis 1:28

11. Cf. Hebrews 2:17; Philippians 2:5–8

12. Cf. Pope Pius XI, encyclical *Quadragesimo Anno*: AAS 23 (1931), p. 221

13. Deuteronomy 24:15; James 5:4; and also Genesis 4:10

14. Cf. Genesis 1:28

15. Cf. Genesis 1:26–27

16. Genesis 3:19

17. Hebrews 6:8; cf. Genesis 3:18

18. Cf. *Summa Theologica*, I-II, q. 40, a. 1, c.; I-II, q. 34, a. 2, ad 1

19. *Ibid.*

20. Cf. *Quadragesimo Anno*: AAS 23 (1931) pp. 221-22

21. Cf. John 4:38

22. On the right to property see *Summa Theologica*, II-II, q. 66, arts. 2 and 6; *De Regimine Principum*, Book 1, Chapters 15 and 17. On the social function of property see *Summa Theologica*, II-II, q. 134, art. 1, ad 3

23. Cf. *Quadragesimo Anno*: AAS 23 (1931), p. 199, Second Vatican Council, *Gaudium et Spes*, 68

24. Cf. Pope John XXIII, encyclical *Mater et Magistra*: AAS 53 (1961), p. 419

25. Cf. *Summa Theologica*, II-II, q. 65, a.2

26. *Gaudium et Spes*, 67

27. *Gaudium et Spes*, 34

28. Cf. Genesis 2:2; Exodus 20:8, 11; Deuteronomy 5:12–14

29. Cf. Genesis 2:3

30. Revelation 15:3

31. Genesis 1:4, 10, 12, 18, 21, 25, 31

32. John 5:17

33. Cf. Hebrews 4:1, 9–10

34. John 14:2

35. Cf. Deuteronomy 5:12–14; Exodus 20:8–12

36. Cf. Matthew 25:21

37. *Gaudium et Spes*, 34

38. *Ibid.*

39. Second Vatican Council, Dogmatic Constitution on the Church, *Lumen Gentium*, 36

40. Mark 6:2–3

41. Cf. Matthew 13:55

42. Cf. Matthew 6:25–34

43. John 15:1

44. Cf. Sirach 38:1–3

45. Cf. Sirach 38:4–8

46. Cf. Exodus 31:1–5; Sirach 38:27

47. Cf. Genesis 4:22; Isaiah 44:12

48. Cf. Jeremiah 18:3–4; Sirach 38:29–30

49. Cf. Genesis 9:20; Isaiah 5:1–2

50. Cf. Ecclesiastes 12:9–12; Sirach 39:1–8

51. Cf. Psalm 107 (108):23–30; Wisdom 14:2–3a

52. Cf. Genesis 11:3; 2 Kings 12:12–13; 22:5–6

53. Cf. Genesis 4:21

54. Cf. Genesis 4:2; 37:3; Exodus 3:1; 1 Samuel 16:11; *et passim*

55. Cf. Ezekiel 47:10

56. Cf. Proverbs 31:15–27

57. E.g., John 10:1–16

58. Cf. Mark 12:1–12

59. Cf. Luke 4:23

60. Cf. Mark 4:1–9

61. Cf. Matthew 13:52

62. Cf. Matthew 24:45; Luke 12:42–48

63. Cf. Luke 16:1–8

64. Cf. Matthew 13:47–50

65. Cf. Matthew 13:45–46

66. Cf. Matthew 20:1–16

67. Cf. Matthew 13:33; Luke 15:8–9

68. Cf. Matthew 9:37; John 4:35–38

69. Cf. Matthew 4:19

70. Cf. Matthew 13:52

71. Cf. Acts of the Apostles 18:3

72. Acts of the Apostles 20:34–35

73. 2 Thessalonians 3:8. St. Paul recognizes that missionaries have a right to their keep: 1 Corinthians 9:6–14; Galatians 6:6; 2 Thessalonians 3:9; cf. Luke 10:7

74. 2 Thessalonians 3:12

75. 2 Thessalonians 3:11

76. 2 Thessalonians 3:10

77. Colossians 3:23–24

78. Cf. Acts of the Apostles 1:1

79. *Gaudium et Spes*, 35

80. *Ibid.*

81. Genesis 3:17

82. Genesis 3:19

83. Ecclesiastes 2:11

84. Cf. Romans 5:19

85. Cf. John 17:4

86. Cf. Luke 9:23

87. *Gaudium et Spes*, 38

88. Cf. 2 Peter 3:13; Revelation 21:1

89. Cf. 2 Peter 3:13

90. *Gaudium et Spes*, 39

91. *Ibid.*

Jubilee of Workers

Homily of Pope John Paul II
(May 1, 2000)

Lord, Give Success to the Work of Our Hands

"Lord, give success to the work of our hands." (Responsorial Psalm)

These words, the refrain in the Responsorial Psalm, clearly express the meaning of today's Jubilee. Today, May 1, a united prayer rises from the vast and multifaceted world of work: Lord, bless us and strengthen the work of our hands!

Our labors—at home, in the fields, in industries, and in offices—could turn into an exhausting busyness ultimately devoid of meaning (cf. Ecclesiastes 1:3). Let us ask the Lord for it [instead] to be the fulfilment of God's plan, so that our work may recover its original meaning.

And what is the original meaning of work? We have heard it in the first reading from the Book of Genesis. God gave us, created in his image and likeness, a command: "Fill the earth and subdue it" (1:28). The Apostle Paul echoes these words when he writes to the Christians of Thessalonica: "When we were with you, we gave you this command: If any one will not work, let him not eat," and exhorts them "to do their work in quietness and to earn their own living" (2 Thessalonians 3:10, 12).

In God's plan, work is therefore seen as a right and duty. Necessary to make the earth's resources benefit the life of each person and of society, work helps to direct human activity toward God in the fulfilment of his command to "subdue the earth." In this regard another of the Apostle Paul's exhortations echoes in our souls: "So, whether you eat or drink, or whatever you do, do all to the glory of God" (1 Corinthians 10:31).

While the Jubilee year [2000] turns our gaze to the mystery of the Incarnation, it invites us to reflect with particular intensity on the hidden life of Jesus in Nazareth. It was there that he spent most of his earthly life. With his silent diligence in Joseph's workshop, Jesus gave the highest proof of the dignity of work. Today's gospel mentions how the residents of Nazareth, his fellow villagers, welcomed him with surprise, asking one another: "Where did this man get this wisdom and these mighty works? Is not this the carpenter's son?" (Matthew 13:54–55).

The Son of God did not disdain being called a "carpenter" and did not want to be spared the normal condition of every human being. "The eloquence of the life of Christ is unequivocal: he belongs to the 'working world,' he has appreciation and respect for human work. It can indeed be said that he looks with love upon human work and the different forms that it takes, seeing in each one of these forms a particular facet of our likeness with God, the Creator and Father" (*Laborem Exercens*).

The teaching of the apostles and of the church derives from Christ's gospel; a true and proper Christian spirituality of work flows from it and was eminently expressed in the Second Vatican Ecumenical Council's Constitution *Gaudium et Spes*. After centuries of heated social and ideological tensions, the contemporary world, ever more interdependent, needs this "gospel of work" so that human activity can promote the authentic development of individuals and of all humanity.

Dear brothers and sisters, who today represent this entire working world gathered for this Jubilee celebration, what does the Jubilee say to you? What does the Jubilee say to society, for which work is not only a fundamental structure but also a proving ground for its choices of value and culture?

Since its Hebrew origins, the Jubilee has directly concerned the reality of work, since the people of God were a people of free men and women redeemed by the Lord from their condition as slaves (cf. Leviticus 25). In the paschal mystery, Christ also brings to fulfilment this institution of the old law, giving it full spiritual meaning but integrating its social dimension into the great plan of the kingdom, which, like leaven, causes the whole of society to make true progress.

Therefore the Jubilee Year calls for a rediscovery of the meaning and value of work. It is also an invitation to address the economic and social imbalances in the world of work by re-establishing the right hierarchy of values, giving priority to the dignity of working men and women and to their freedom, responsibility, and participation. It also spurs us to redress situations of injustice by safeguarding each people's culture and different models of development.

At this moment I cannot fail to express my solidarity with all who are suffering because of unemployment, inadequate wages, or lack of material resources. I am well aware of the people who are reduced to a poverty that offends their dignity, prevents them from sharing the earth's goods, and obliges them to eat whatever scraps fall from the tables of the rich (cf. Bull of Indiction *Incarnationis Mysterium*). The effort to remedy these situations is a labor of justice and peace.

The new realities that are having such a powerful impact on the productive process, such as the globalization of finance, economics, trade, and labor, must never violate the dignity and centrality of the human person, nor the freedom and democracy of peoples. If solidarity, participation, and the possibility to manage these radical changes are not the [total] solution, they are certainly the necessary ethical guarantee so that individuals and people do not become tools but the protagonists of their future. All this can be achieved and, since it is possible, it becomes a duty.

The Pontifical Council for Justice and Peace is reflecting on these themes and is closely following developments in the world's economic and social situation, in order to study their effects on the human being. The result of this reflection will be the *Compendium of the Social Doctrine of the Church*, which is now being compiled [and was released in 2005].

Dear workers, our meeting is illumined by the figure of Joseph of Nazareth and by his spiritual and moral stature, as lofty as it is humble and discreet. The promise of the Psalm is fulfilled in him: "Blessed is every one who fears the Lord, who walks in his ways. You shall eat the fruit of the labor of your hands; you shall be happy, and it shall be well with you....Thus shall people be blessed who fear the Lord" (127:1–2, 4). The Guardian of the Redeemer taught Jesus the carpenter's trade, but above all he set him the most valuable example of what Scripture calls the "fear of God," the very beginning of wisdom, which consists in religious submission to him and in the deep desire to seek and always carry out his will. This, dear friends, is the true source of blessing for every person, for every family, and for every nation.

I entrust all of you and your families to St. Joseph, a worker and just man, and to his most holy wife, Mary.

"Lord, give success to the work of our hands."

Bless, O Lord of the centuries and the millennia, the daily work by which men and women provide bread for themselves and their loved ones. We also offer to your hands the toil and sacrifices associated with work, in union with your Son Jesus Christ, who redeemed human work from the yoke of sin and restored it to its original dignity. To you be praise and glory today and for ever. Amen.

OF RELATED INTEREST

The Lord's Day
Reflections on Dies Domini, the Apostolic Letter of Pope John Paul II

Here's a wonderful little book for every member of your parish. In it, Pope John Paul II shares why Sunday is such a special day in our Christian tradition and how it can change our lives if we let it. He invites us to slow down, to think, to pray, to reach out to God in a special way—in a word, to let Sunday truly be Sunday.
32 pages • 99¢ • 95-623-6

Walking in the Light
30 Days with Pope John Paul II

Each of the Pope's daily reflections centers on a Christian virtue and is meant to be prayerfully pondered, read and re-read, until it takes root in the reader's heart. These thirty days with Pope John Paul II inspire us to embrace the Christian life more fully so that the light of Christ can shine brightly through us to all the world. Color photos throughout.
72 pages • hardcover • $9.95 • 95-382-2

Walking in Faith
30 Days with Pope Benedict XVI

These brief spiritual messages from Pope Benedict XVI offer insights about what it means to be a Catholic believer. Each of these daily reflections is simple, challenging, heartfelt, and uplifting, and each is accompanied by a Scripture passage, a prayer, and an action response to the pope's daily challenge to "walk in faith."
32 pages • 99¢ • 95-544-2

Walking in Love
30 Days with the Encyclical "God Is Love" from Pope Benedict XVI

Our Holy Father has chosen love as the topic for his first encyclical, his first "letter to the world." Why love? He explains that the statement "God is love" is at the very heart of our faith. It touches everything we are and everything we do. Being a Christian, he says, is the result of our astonishing encounter with God—who first loved us.
32 pages • 99¢ • 95-595-7

TO ORDER CALL 1-800-321-0411 OR
VISIT **www.23rdpublications.com**